A Study Skills Handbook

A Study Skills Handbook

Mike and Glenda Smith

OXFORD
UNIVERSITY PRESS

Oxford University Press
Great Clarendon Street, Oxford OX2 6DP

Oxford New York
Athens Auckland Bangkok Bogota Bombay
Buenos Aires Calcutta Cape Town Dar es Salaam
Delhi Florence Hong Kong Istanbul Karachi
Kuala Lumpur Madras Madrid Melbourne
Mexico City Nairobi Paris Singapore
Taipei Tokyo Toronto Warsaw

and associated companies in
Berlin Ibadan

OXFORD and OXFORD ENGLISH are trade marks of
Oxford University Press

ISBN 0 19 451226 6

© Mike and Glenda Smith 1990

First published 1988
Second edition 1990
Ninth impression 1998

Printed in China

Contents

PRESENTING YOUR INFORMATION

Acknowledgements

We wish to thank Dr Bill Schreck for allowing us to pilot the first drafts of many of the units on the Foundation English Course at the University of Papua New Guinea. Dr Schreck must also be thanked for introducing us to the approach to writing argumentative essays originally developed by Kenneth A. Bruffee in 1980 in *A Short Course in Writing*, Winthrop, USA. We have simplified somewhat Bruffee's approach in this book.

We also thank the following people who provided specialist material for the units from their own courses: Professor Maeve O'Collins (who also provided advice in the original stages of the descriptive essay unit), for sociology; Professor John Lynch for linguistics; Duncan Colquon-Kerr for law; Kevin Darcy for general studies; Peter Smith for education; Dr Tom Wyatt for materials on psychology.

We also wish to thank Catherine de Courcy of the Library of the University of Papua New Guinea for her help in making available for copying the originals of the books and journals.

The following people provided valuable advice and criticism during the early stages of the writing: John Davani, Pat Hardy, Litha Pataki-Schweizer, Ganga Powel, Dr Howard Van Trease, Metone Wamma, Apoi Yarapea.

The materials were trialled at the University of Papua New Guinea and at the College of Allied Health Sciences, Port Moresby. To the students of both these institutions who worked through early drafts of the units, we extend our warmest thanks. Without them, many of the pitfalls of the original materials would still be in the book.

Mike and Glenda Smith

The authors and publisher thank copyright holders for permission to reproduce copyright material from the following:

Arden Library: Ida C. Ward, *The Phonetics of English* (W. Heffer & Sons Ltd, 1962), p. 38; Basil Blackwell Ltd: Colin Gill, *Work, Unemployment and the New Technology* (1985), pp. 65, 66, and J. Gretton & A. Harrison, *How Much Are Public Servants Worth?* (1982), pp. 63, 64; Butterworths: J. P. Cole, *Geography of World Affairs* (6th edn, 1983), pp. 131, 134, 136; Clarendon Press: Peter Earle (ed.), *Essays in European Economic History, 1500–1800* (1974), pp. 200–1, and Olivia Smith, *The Politics of Language 1791–1819* (1984), pp. 153, 154; *Discover* (Dec. 1986), pp. 111–13; *Economist* (28 March 1987), p. 82, (18 April 1987), p. 84; *Far Eastern Economic Review* (2 August 1984), pp. 73–8, 125, 126; *Geographical Magazine* (July 1986), pp. 67, 68; Hart-Davis Ltd: F. C. Cartwright, *Disease and History* (1972), pp. 58, 59–60; Longman Group Ltd: J. A. Bright & G. P. McGregor, *Teaching English as a Second Language* (1970), pp. 194–5; Macmillan Publishers Ltd: Alan S. Milward, *The Economic Effects of the Two World Wars on Britain* (1984), pp. 177–8. Tom McArthur, *The Written Word*, Book 2 (1987), pp. 196–7; Millenium Publishing Group: *Millenium: Journal of International Studies*, vol. 15, no. 1 (1986), pp. 179–80; *New Internationalist*, no. 89 (1980), pp. 158–60, 166–7, no. 90 (1980), pp. 168–71; *New Scientist* (18 July 1985), pp. 106, 107, (22 January 1987), p. 70, (2 April 1987) p. 80; Oxford University Press, Kuala Lumpur: Ooi Jin Bee, *The Petroleum Resources of Indonesia* (1982), pp. 96–8; Oxford University Press, Oxford: W. A. Eltis, & P. J. N. Sinclair, *The Money Supply and the Exchange Rate* (1981), pp. 186–7, J. E. King, *Readings in Labour Economics* (1980), pp. 188–9, Janet Ramage, *Energy: A Guidebook* (1983), pp. 198–9; and D. A. Wilkins, *Notional Syllabuses* (1976), pp. 182–3, *ELT Journal*, vol. 39, no. 1 (1985), pp. 99–100, vol. 43, no. 3, pp. 42–3, and *Oxford Economic Papers*, vol. 37 (June 1985), p. 192; Pergamon Press: *Energy Journal*, vol. 11, no. 6 (1986), p. 193; Polynesian Society Inc.: *Journal of the Polynesian Society*, vol. 95, no. 4 (1986), pp. 190–1; Royal Australian Historical Society, *Journal of the Royal Australian Historical Society*, vol. 72, part 2 (October 1986), p. 155; Society of Chemical Industry: *Journal of the Science of Food and Agriculture*, vol. 38, no. 3 (1987), pp. 202–3; University of Adelaide: *Australian Economic Papers*, vol. 24, no. 45 (1985), p. 181; University of Queensland Press: John Hill, *From Subservience to Strike* (1982), pp. 175–6; World Health Organization, Geneva, Switzerland: *World Health* (Aug./Sept. 1986), pp. 86–7.

Disclaimer

Every effort has been made to trace the original source of all copyright material contained in this book. The authors and publisher would be pleased to hear from copyright holders to rectify any errors or omissions.

Introduction

PART 1

Introduction for the Student

This course is designed to help you become a successful student. It has been written for students whose mother tongue is not English, yet who, for one reason or another, are completing a course of study where English is the only language of instruction. If you are such a student, we hope that this course will help you achieve the most from your studies.

If you look quickly through the book, you will see that this is not just a course that talks about studying: it is a workbook that expects you to practise the skills as you go along. We have written the course in the form of a workbook for a very good reason: studying is a very complex skill, and, like all other skills, it needs practice. You cannot learn to drive a car or fly an aeroplane just by reading a book: and you cannot become an efficient student by only reading about how to do it.

Because the skill of studying is so complex, it is almost impossible to split the task into a number of neat 'units' covering different aspects. That is why you will find frequent mention of work done in earlier units of the book, or even mention of work that will be covered in later ones. Wherever mention is made of past units, look quickly back to the relevant section to check that you remember what it was all about. If you do this, you will understand more quickly the point of the new section you are about to begin. If you look at Index 1 at the back of this book, you will find a list of the places where units are linked together in this way.

One of the biggest problems facing anyone learning a new skill is so-called 'transference'. This means that everyone has problems transferring the newly acquired skill from one course to another. In the case of study skills this means that students have difficulty applying what is learnt in the language class to what is expected by specialist subject lecturers. To help you avoid this problem, we have tried to link the study skills as closely as possible to the other major courses you are studying: we have done this by suggesting at various crucial points that you try to apply the current skill to the work you are doing in your major subjects. This is a very important part of the course, and it is one that you should try to be most conscientious about. If you fail to make the links, then you will not transfer your skills properly.

This course is designed to be part of a taught course in an educational institution, and for this reason refers frequently to the tutor or lecturer. You can work through this course without a teacher, and gain a great deal from it; but, if you do decide to work through this without a teacher, try to persuade someone else to work through it at the same time. If you work with a partner on many of the exercises, you will both learn a great deal more than if you try to go through the whole thing on your own. It is also much more fun!

Glenda Smith

PART 2

Introduction for the Teacher

Some years ago at the end of a lesson on reading skills, one of my Singaporean teacher–trainees came up to me and said, 'Mr Smith, I can read everything I'm asked to, and I can understand all the words, so why is it that I can never work out what the main points are?' At the time I had no answer for him, as I was still fairly new to ESL teaching: coming as I had from years of EFL teaching,* it seemed to me more than enough that the students could read English with any fluency at all.

It was only when I heard almost the exactly the same words from a Melanesian student in Papua New Guinea that I began to look more closely into the problem. When I did look, I realized just how difficult a task we were asking our ESL students to carry out. It quickly became obvious that, to help students' reading skills, it was not enough just to tell them to read for the main points. Before they could do that, they needed to be able understand how the reading passages were put together: and the best way to teach them that was to teach them to *write* in that way. Before they could write in that way, they needed other skills . . . And so the project grew.

After three years of work, and a lot of trial and error, this book is the result. We hope it goes some way towards answering those two students.

This is a workbook of study skills, and, as such, is intended to provide practical work for students in classroom and tutorial. The units in the course have been extensively trialled in two institutions: the University of Papua New Guinea, and the College of Allied Health Services in Port Moresby. We therefore feel that this course will be suitable for a wide range of students with different backgrounds.

The main thrust behind the course is to increase students' efficiency in their academic work by giving them practice in basic techniques. For this reason many of the units are very proscriptive in their approach. This has been done quite deliberately, for we feel that many of our students lack a solid foundation to build on. We would suggest that the units are taught as they stand, and that

---

* ESL—English as a Second Language; EFL—English as a Foreign Language.

only after the relevant unit is completed should students be encouraged to develop their own personal style. This is particularly true of Unit 6: Part 3, Writing an Essay, which attempts to give students practice in putting together a 'logical' argument.

It is also true of Unit 7: Quoting Skills, where only one method of writing a bibliography is covered. We have reached the somewhat cynical conclusion that no two academics have the same system of laying out bibliographical entries, and that certainly none of them are prepared to accept anyone else's system. We have chosen one technique, and have taught that, working on the principle that, provided the students have a grasp of the basic principles, minor differences can be specified by individual lecturers.

We have tried to integrate the course on two levels. First, we have tried to spiral the skills through the units, and second, we have tried to indicate how students can use the skills they are learning in the real world of their major subjects. The latter integration is, of course, very important, and a considerable amount of attention should be paid to this, possibly when the students come to the assignment stage of each unit.

Although the integration of the skills through the units is important, it should not be thought that the units must be taught in the order that they are presented in the book. It may be useful, for instance, to delay Unit 1: Using Your Time, until halfway through the first term, when students are beginning to realize that they have mismanaged their studying and feel that they need help.

If time is limited for the course, some units can be left to the students to work on by themselves, with only the very minimum of tutorial supervision. The following units could be left for students to do on their own:

Unit 1: Using Your Time;
Unit 2: Dictionary Skills;
Unit 5: Notetaking Skills.

In addition, certain parts of some of the units could be left for private study. These are:

Unit 6: Writing Skills (Part 1);
Unit 7: Quoting Skills (Parts 1 and 3).

We have found that some of the units will take much longer than others. This is particularly true of Unit 6: Part 3, Writing an Argumentative Essay.

As this is a course for students whose mother tongue is not English, we have tried to include a great deal of 'disguised' language work in the course. Teachers could extend this language teaching element considerably by adopting the following technique. All written work is marked but not corrected. Instead, mistakes are simply underlined, and a note made in the margin telling the student what kind of mistake has been made (*gr* for grammar, *t* for tense, *sp* for spelling, *awk* for awkwardly written, etc.). Students are then expected to rewrite the piece of work, having worked over the mistakes with a dictionary, and perhaps a grammar book, to find out what is wrong. Marks are only awarded for the final end-of-course assessment if the rewritten work is submitted.

We have found this technique particularly successful, as it encourages accuracy. Students spot most of the mistakes immediately: the rest can be worked out if the teacher has shown students how to use the dictionary properly. The consistent use of example sentences in each dictionary entry is invaluable for this, as it shows permissible collocations or any word students are likely to use.

Mike Smith

UNIT 1

Using Your Time

PART 1

Establishing a Routine

A full-time course of study is different from any other form of work in one major way: in any other occupation you have set times to work that keep you busy most of the day. However, apart from the actual times of your lessons and tutorials, there are no set working hours in an academic course. It is up to you to choose what you will do with the time available. No one will tell you what to do, or when to do it.

This is a very grave responsibility to yourself, for the only person who will tell you what to do and when to do it is you yourself. It is up to you alone to decide how to use your time wisely. If you mismanage your time, you will have only yourself to blame.

If you do not organize your time wisely, you will not get the most out of your study. Ironically, whether you spend none of your time studying, or if you spend all of your time studying, the results will be the same: you will not be a successful student.

The student who spends every spare minute in the library trying to cram information into his brain is little better in the end than the student who has spent an absolute minimum of time in the library, and the rest of the time on the sports field. Neither of them will do as well in their academic studies as they should have done, for neither of them will have managed the time properly.

Successful graduates of any academic institution are people who have succeeded in organizing themselves in such a way that they have realized their full potential as students.

A point to bear in mind: no matter what your previous experience—be it years of work, or merely time at secondary school—employers welcome a good pass in any academic examination, such as national examinations, a specialist diploma or a university degree, because this tells an employer that you are able to work on your own and to make the most efficient use of the time available.

EXERCISE 1.1

The chances are that you are already worried about your work. What worries you most?

Look at the list below and try to decide which of the statements apply to you. Write down each one that you feel represents your own problems.

1 I don't think I work hard enough.

2 I put in lots of hours last week, but I didn't achieve anything.

3 I find it takes me a long time to get down to work.

4 I don't seem to be able to stick to a task for long.

5 Nearly everyone works harder than I do.

6 I find it difficult to talk to others about the work I'm doing.

7 Nearly everyone seems to know more about the courses than I do.

8 I don't know if I'm doing enough or too much.

9 I can't seem to get much done in the afternoons.

10 I feel guilty every time I spend an evening away from my books.

11 Some weeks I work very hard, but some weeks I don't seem to do anything.

12 I'm always behind everyone else in my work.

13 I don't see how I can ever cover all the work I'm expected to.

14 I don't know what order I should do things in.

15 I'm not sure I shall ever be able to keep going until the end of the course.

a Look at your neighbour's responses. Has he or she written down the same things as you did?

b Between the two of you, decide which five problems in the list worry you most. Write them down.

Discuss these with your tutor and with the rest of the class.

Making a Study Timetable

The first and most important thing you must do as a professional student is to **plan your working week.** The only way you can ever hope to make the most efficient use of your time is to plan it as carefully as you can. You must make a timetable for yourself and stick to it! If you set yourself tasks that are planned out hour by hour, day by day, you will achieve far more than you could ever hope to do by simply flitting from task to task like an insect on a flowering bush.

There are several golden rules that you should follow when you make your timetable.

GOLDEN RULE—1

Establish a daily routine.

A   Try to pace yourself, working regularly each day.

Your brain is a muscle, not very different from the other muscles in your body. It performs best if you subject it to a regular rhythm. Think of two people climbing a steep hill. The one who gets to the top fastest is the one who establishes a steady, regular pace. The one who runs as hard as he can until he drops and then rests, only to rush on again, takes much longer to get there if he ever gets there at all!

Answer the following questions about yourself—truthfully! If you reply truthfully, you will have learned something about your work rhythm which will be useful when you come to plan your weekly study timetable.

1 How often in an hour do you feel the need to get up and stretch your legs while you are reading a textbook?

2 At what time of the day do you work best?
(a) morning
(b) afternoon
(c) evening
(d) late at night

3 Write down the hours when you can study *at the same time every day in the week* (meal times and travel times do not count!).

B   Try to study in the same place each day.

Do not go to different places each time, or you will waste a lot of time looking around, staring at the view out of the window, and so on. If you always sit at the same desk in the library, for example, you will not be distracted by new things. Also, your mind will establish an association between your regular desk and work; this means that, before long, your brain will automatically prepare itself for work when you sit down.

Answer the following questions about the places where you work—be honest! Which are the places where you feel happiest working? Why do you prefer these places?

C   Do not try to study for long periods of time without a rest.

It is important to work hard while you are actually at your best, but it is just as important to allow your brain time to rest and relax fairly regularly. No one can concentrate for extended periods of time.

Allow yourself a ten-minute break every hour. Go for a stroll round the building, have a look at the newspaper or just go and sit under a tree. When you take one of these breaks, make it a real break: do not keep thinking about what you have been reading. It will all still be there when you get back to your seat.

If what you are doing involves a great deal of concentration, give yourself a major break every two hours: go and have a cup of coffee, or have something to eat. Once again, try to let your mind concern itself with something other than the book you have been concentrating on.

D   Give yourself *at least* half a day off each week.

During this time, do not think about your work. Think about anything else. Your brain needs a regular holiday, just as much as you do!

Answer these questions about your free time:
When in the week do you have a half a day without commitments?
Which of the times you have written would be best for your half-day rest?

GOLDEN RULE—2

Set yourself easily attainable goals.

A Do not set yourself a task that you cannot finish in the time available.

You wouldn't sit down in a two-hour break between lectures and try to read a 300-page book—or would you? That would obviously be a thoroughly unreasonable thing to do, and at the end of the two hours you would be frustrated by the fact that you had not achieved what you set out to do.

One of the most useful things you can do is to limit what you want to achieve in a set study period to something that you can *easily* get completed. In that way you will always finish what you set out to do, and by the end of a day or week you will be able to relax, knowing that you are keeping up with your schedule.

An effective student is a happy student, and you are at your happiest when you are achieving what you originally set out to do!

Answer the following questions about things that affect your planning:
1 How long does it take you to read ten pages of a textbook?
2 How long does it take you to read ten pages of a novel?
3 How long does it take you to write a two-page class paper?
    Discuss your conclusions with a partner. Are you both being *realistic*? Are you being *honest*?

In the light of what you have written down, complete the following exercise.

EXERCISE 1.2

Imagine you have scheduled yourself for an hour's work in the library. Which of these tasks should you take up?

1 Reading through the morning's lecture notes.
2 Writing that overdue 3000-word assignment.
3 Looking for books on your next assignment.
4 Writing a one-page assignment for tomorrow.
5 Reading a 10-page journal article.
6 Reading a 15-page journal article.
7 Proofreading your latest assignment for English errors.
8 Revising a first draft of that 3000-word assignment.
9 Having an afternoon nap.

Discuss with a partner how long each one would take.

    If you finish your work earlier than you intended, then that is so much the better. It means that you have 'won' some free time. Do not be tempted to start something you will not be able to finish, or else you will end up frustrated all over again!

B Define your goals as precisely as possible.

EXERCISE 1.3

Look at these examples of what needs to be done.
  Which of the tasks is the most precisely outlined? Which is the least precisely outlined?
1 Read *Education in the Third World*.
2 Make notes on chapter 3 of *Education in the Third World* especially about community/primary schools.
3 Read and take notes on *Education in the Third World*.
4 Make notes on chapter 3 of *Education in the Third World*.
5 Have a look at that book on education . . .

It is much easier to achieve goals that are clearly defined. Be as detailed as possible. The more detailed you make your goal, the better. The other advantage of defining goals is that it will force you to decide why it is that you are reading the book at all!

REMEMBER: The first rule about reading anything for information is that you must have clearly in your mind the *reason why* you are looking at the book.

GOLDEN RULE—3

Recognize your own strengths and weaknesses and build them into your timetable.

It is no good writing out a timetable that you will not be able to keep to, even on the first day.

You must try to build in your own shortcomings as well as your own strengths. For instance, if you work best early in the morning, it is silly to give yourself the morning free and put yourself in the library every afternoon, when you are at your worst.

When you plan your timetable, you must take into account all the other factors that you have been looking at in this unit. These are:
1 the hours when you have lessons and tutorials;
2 meal times—be fair with yourself here: do not give yourself twenty minutes to do what normally takes an hour!;
3 the times when you work best—schedule your hardest studying into these times;
4 rest periods—allow yourself free time on a regular basis.

Answer the following questions about the times in the week when you cannot study.

EXERCISE 1.4

1 How long do you spend over
   (a) breakfast?   (c) evening meal?
   (b) lunch?   (d) drinks during the day?

2 How many hours do you need to sleep each night in order to wake up refreshed the following morning?

3 Are there any other regular commitments that you should take into account when planning a week's work? (Church attendance may be one, games practice may be another.)

If you take all these things into account, you should end up with a workable timetable—and that is what all this is about!

Look at the extract from a university student's timetable below. Are there any criticisms you would make of it?

	Monday	Tuesday	Wednesday	Thursday	Friday	Saturday	Sunday
7–8	study	study	study		study	study	study
8–9	LECTURE	LECTURE			study	study	CHURCH
9–10	LECTURE	LECTURE		LECTURE	LECTURE	study	study
10–11	study	LECTURE	LECTURE	TUTORIAL	LECTURE	study	study
11–12	study	study	TUTORIAL		study	study	study
12–1	study	study			LECTURE	study	study
1–2	TUTORIAL	study	FOOTBALL	LECTURE	study	FOOTBALL	study
2–3	study	TUTORIAL	FOOTBALL	LECTURE	SHOPPING IN TOWN	FOOTBALL	study
3–4	TUTORIAL	TUTORIAL	study	LECTURE	study	study	study
4–5	study	study	study		study	study	study
5–6	study	study	study		study	study	study
6–7	EVENING MEAL TIME						
7–8	study	free	write letters	study	study	study	study
8–9	study	study	study	study	study	study	study
9–10	study	study	study	study	study	study	study
10–11	study	study	study	study	study	study	study

Now prepare for yourself a blank timetable like the one below. **Make a copy of this time-table blank**. Fill in your own timetable for this term on one copy. The second copy is for your revised version of this timetable, which you should make in about two weeks' time. By then you will have encountered the unworkable parts of this, your first timetable. Put the revised version on the wall of your room.

Make sure you use it!

PROVISIONAL STUDY TIMETABLE FOR TERM ____

	Monday	Tuesday	Wednesday	Thursday	Friday	Saturday	Sunday
7–8							
8–9							
9–10							
10–11							
11–12							
12–1							
1–2							
2–3							
3–4							
4–5							
5–6							
6–7							
7–8							
8–9							
9–10							
10–11							

UNIT 2

Dictionary Skills

These exercises on dictionary work are based on the two leading dictionaries for speakers of English as a second language: the *Oxford Advanced Learner's Dictionary*, edited by A.P. Cowie, Oxford University Press 1989, and the *Longman Dictionary of Contemporary English*, edited by Paul Procter, Longman 1987. You will not be able to do these exercises without one of these dictionaries.

When it is necessary to refer to one of these dictionaries in particular, this will be done by using the following initials:

OALD means the Oxford dictionary
LDOCE means the Longman dictionary.

Both OALD and LDOCE are designed to help you to speak, write and read English more efficiently. They contain information not just about spelling, but also about pronunciation, shades of meaning, grammar and style. Because of their compact layout, some of the information may seem difficult to grasp at first, that is why exercises such as those in this book are necessary and worthwhile. Your dictionary is an essential tool for you, both now as a student and later in your professional life. The aim of these exercises is to make you familiar with the very wide range of information available in your dictionary and to give you practice in finding the information speedily and accurately.

REMEMBER: The more you use your dictionary, the more uses you will find for it!

Because these exercises have been designed specifically for use with OALD and LDOCE, the answers to all the questions are there in your dictionary for you to find. You should be able to check your work yourself and not have to rely on a teacher to provide the answers. It is important to develop the habit of checking if you want to improve your command of any language. Even if you think you know the answer, or you want to make an inspired guess, always look up the relevant entry to double check—then you will be sure you are right, and you will probably learn some extra information at the same time.

The benefit you gain from these exercises and from your dictionary will be in direct proportion to the amount of effort you invest.

PART 1

Finding Your Way Around the Dictionary

Your dictionary is crammed with various kinds of information. Before we begin, open it and look at what is inside.

Look at the inside covers. What are the headings at the top of the pages at the front of the book? What are the headings on the pages at the back of the book?

Now look for the sections that cover the following topics. Write down what the dictionary calls each section and the page number that section starts on.

Note that the sections may be in the front or in the back of the book.

1 Where to find out *how the entries work*
2 Where to find a list of the *abbreviations used in the dictionary*
3 Where to find a list of *weights and measures*
4 Where to find help with *how to pronounce a word*
5 Where to find a list of *irregular verbs*

These are some of the points that are dealt with in the dictionary. The list of Contents will show you just what else there is. The aim of our book is to make you familiar with as many of these sections as possible, so that you can use the dictionary effectively.

Finding Words Quickly

There are many thousands of entries in your dictionary, and you will become frustrated if you cannot quickly find the word you need. The entries are arranged alphabetically, so before you open the book to find a word, *think about it*: where will the word be? Will it be in the back? in the middle? at the front?

EXERCISE 2.1

a By picking up the dictionary and *thinking* before you open it, see how close you can get to the following words:

    X-ray   manger   brink   taro

b Open your dictionary somewhere in the middle. At the top of each page you will see two words printed in heavy type. The word on the left is the first word on the page, and the one on the right is the last word on that page. These words can be a great help when you are trying to find a particular word quickly. Use them as guides to what can be found on a page.

EXERCISE 2.2

a Practice finding individual words as quickly as possible.

Locate the following words—you should be able to find each one before you have counted to ten. Write down the words which appear at the top of the page.

   specimen   organism   adapt   various

If you find this difficult to do within the time limit, give yourself some more practice by looking up any word at random—try the words in this sentence if you like! Keep practising until you can find any word before you have counted to ten.

b Look at the following example.

If the two words on a page are 'leg' and 'letter', only the **bold** words in the following list would appear on that page:

   let   **lesson**   law   last   list   **lend**

Decide which of the following words would appear between the guide words given, and write them down:

1 **authenticity/avoid**

average	avoidance	autograph
authoress	authentic	auxiliary

2 **incur/indirect**

indignity	index	induct
incursion	incubus	inconvenient

3 **pass/paste**

part	past	passion
paternal	poem	pate

4 **sea going/sec**

searing	seaworthy	seductive
scrubby	sea anemone	security

5 **task/teak**

teahouse	taxi	tango
tarn	telegram	taste

6 **bilberry/birdie**

biplane	biography	birth
bilateral	bikini	bingo

PART 2

Using the Dictionary's Special Abbreviations and Punctuation

Abbreviations

Abbreviations are used in the dictionary to save space. It will save you time if you know what they stand for. The information is inside the front cover of the dictionary. Of course you must know what the full word means too, so, if one of the words in the list in the front cover is not familiar to you, **look it up** so that you will understand what is meant when it is used in a dictionary entry.

EXERCISE 2.3

Write down the full word for these abbreviations.

REMEMBER: If you do not know the meaning of any of the words that you copy from the front of the dictionary, look it up!

esp	infml	neg	sl
fem	Lat	pl	usu
euph	masc	reflex	US

Every entry in the dictionary uses certain abbreviations to indicate what 'part of speech' a word is (in other words, how the word can be used).

EXERCISE 2.4

Write down the full word for the following abbreviations for parts of speech, and give an example for each one. If you cannot think of an example, the dictionary will give you one when you look it up under the entry for the full word. Write your answer like this (see p. 22):

Abbreviation	Full word	Example
infin adj adv aux conj suff pron prep	infinitive	*Allow him to go*

All these abbreviations come at the beginning of the explanation for each word (this explanation is called an entry).

EXERCISE 2.5

Look up the entry for the following words, and write down the *grammatical abbreviations* used after them:

e.g.   saturate   v
     vinegar
     honestly
     sanguine
     myself
     although
     a^2

EXERCISE 2.6

Often there is more than one entry in the dictionary for one word. For instance, look up 'glare'. You will find two entries in your dictionary: **glare**[1], and **glare**[2]. Don't be confused between the numbers *beside* the headword (**glare**[2]) and the numbers *inside* the entry (**glare**[2] ...**1**...**2**...). In the case of **glare**, one of the headwords is a *noun* and one is a *verb*.

Write down which *entry* for **glare** is the right one for the following examples:

> The glare of the sun on the water.
> The sun glared down on us all day.

If you look carefully at the sample sentences given for each of the two entries, you will be able to see which is which.

Now try the following examples:

1 **low**
a low table
Stocks of food ran low.
The stockmarket reached a new low.
The cattle lowed in the field.

2 **register**
a cash register
a registered letter

3 **sound**
a sound mind
the sound of voices
They sounded the alarm.
The ship sounded the channel.

4 **spring**
a hot spring
He springs to attention.

5 **subject**
an Australian subject
to subject oneself to criticism
a subject people

6 **there**
There now, what did I tell you?
We're nearly there.
There's no stopping him.

7 **will**
I believe in free will.
We will pay it back soon.
God has willed it.
Come whenever you will.

8 **faint**
Faint traces were visible.
He fainted from hunger.

As you will have seen from the previous exercise, words that 'look the same' often have different grammatical functions. For example, 'mortal' can be (a) an adjective (adj) as in 'a *mortal* wound', (b) a noun (n) as in 'We are all *mortals*'.

When a word can be used as different parts of speech, the dictionary indicates this by either using a new headword, e.g. **glare**[2], or by using a triangle △.

Look at the relevant page in the guide to using the dictionary where this is explained.

EXERCISE 2.7

Look up the following words, and write down the abbreviations you find for each of them that describes which part of speech they can be.
Then write sentences as examples to illustrate how the part of speech is used.

Example: extract: (a) v He extracted the cork.
          (b) n This food is an extract of malt.

In the dictionary the entry is **extract** (*v*), and then **extract** (*n*).
Do the same with the following words:

relative   heap   this   past

Write down the possible parts of speech and examples for each.

Abbreviations in the entries not only give information about what part of speech a word is, they sometimes also give more general information about where the word comes from or whether its usage is restricted to certain situations or not.

Look up **inchoate** (adj.). It is described as 'formal' (fml). That means it is an adjective and it is used *only* in **formal writing**.

Example: *His ideas were inchoate at that stage.*

In other words, if you use a word like 'inchoate' in general speech, perhaps to a friend, you may be making your English sound strangely formal. It would make you sound like a book!

To a friend you would be more likely to say:

'*His ideas were still only half-formed.*'

Now look up **compos mentis**. The entry for this describes the expression as '*adj* (Lat) (infml)'. This means that *compos mentis* is an adjective, but it can only be used in informal English (which means *spoken* English).

In other words, if you use this in your *written* English you would be sounding very casual, as written English tends to be more formal than that which is spoken. The dictionary gives you an alternative when you want to write *compos mentis*—sane.

EXERCISE 2.8

Look up the following words and write down the abbreviations that are used with them. Do not copy blindly: make sure you understand what is meant each time!

senior citizen	(old person)	skinny	(thin)
geezer	(old man)	suck up to	(make oneself liked)
mead	(meadow)	tripe	(nonsense)

Spelling

Sometimes there is more than one correct way to spell a word in English. The English and the Australians spell certain words differently from the Americans. Either spelling is correct in a given context, but *it is not acceptable* to use a mixture of English and American spelling in the same piece of writing!

You should decide which is appropriate in your situation, and then use that version throughout that piece of writing.

EXERCISE 2.9

Find the alternative British English spelling for these words given in American spelling:

catalog	skillful	jeweler
theater	plow	check-book
color		

Then find the alternative American spelling for the words given in British English spelling:

offence	licence	flavour
manoeuvre	centre	travelling
sceptical		

Special Punctuation

The dictionary often uses special symbols to help you understand all the information it has to give. You should read very carefully the section 'Using the Dictionary—a practical guide' in OALD, and 'Punctuation in the dictionary' in LDOCE before doing the exercise.

EXERCISE 2.10

a Write down two more words that can be made by adding letters to the end of each of the following words.

Remember to look for ~ in LDOCE or ▷ in OALD.

e.g. corrupt
 ▷ corruptible
 corruptibility

1 home
2 quick
3 exaggerate
4 northern

b Write down what you are told to look up in the entry given for each of the following words.

REMEMBER: Look for an arrow or cf., e.g. **few** ⇒ usage at LESS.

1 nave
2 daughter
3 drive
4 bullet

c Write down what kind of *objects* usually go with the following verbs.

REMEMBER: Look for ( ) in the explanation part of the entry, e.g. **debunk** (a person, an idea)

1 compile
2 navigate
3 pasteurize
4 swaddle

d Write down the *word or phrase that can be included or left out* with the following, depending on how the word is used in a sentence.

REMEMBER: Look for **( )** in heavy (**bold**) type, e.g. **depart (for** . . .) (**from** . . .)

1 succumb
2 denude
3 quote
4 conceal

Another important piece of information provided by the dictionary is that it tells you where to *divide* a word if there is not enough room at the end of a line. The dictionary does this by putting a · inside the headword.

Thus **syl·la·ble** can be divided at the end of a line, like this: syl-, or sylla-; but never: syll-, or sy-.

Note: *Never* split a word so that you leave either the first letter on one line or the last letter on the next line.

Example:

syllabl-   s-
e   yllables

These are wrong.

EXERCISE 2.11

a Indicate with a dot (·), as is done in the dictionary, where these words can divided. If they cannot be divided, indicate this with a cross.

Example: formation—**for·ma·tion**.

honourable	obscure
proportion	language
disturbance	bonus
investment	command
productive	busy

b Look at these end-of-line divisions taken from newspapers. It is often very difficult to understand what the words should be. Using your dictionary, rewrite the words indicating with a dot (·) how the newspapers should have divided them.

boo- kends	dinin- groom
spo- kesman	surpri- sed
on- ce	chee- seburger

PART 3

Using the Dictionary's Lexical Information

Before you begin this section, look at the title again. Do you know what 'lexical' means? If you are not sure, *look it up*!

Affixes

In English many words are built up by fixing groups of letters on to the beginning or the end of the word. Such groups of letters are known as **affixes**.

An affix that comes at the beginning of a word is called a **prefix**, and an affix that comes at the end of a word is called a **suffix**.

By getting to know the common affixes you will be able to work out the meaning of words which are new to you.

EXERCISE 2.12

Some prefixes have meanings which are to do with numbers, for example: mono- means 'one', as in monologue, monochrome.

Now find some words which use these prefixes:

e.g. bi = two   quad = four
tri = three   semi = half
poly = many

Now find some that are to do with *time*:

re = again
pre = before
post = after
chron = of time

Now find some to do with *place*:

inter = between
sub = below
intra = inside

EXERCISE 2.13

The following prefixes are used to make a word mean the opposite to its original meaning: dis-, il-, im-, in-, ir-, mis-, non-, un-. Check in the dictionary to make sure you know how each of them is used.

a Write the *opposites* of the words given below:

logical	desirable
illusion	manage
mortal	sensitive
refutable	sense

b When the prefix is removed, a positive form sometimes emerges—but not always!
   Write the positive form of the words given below by removing the prefix—but only when possible. Where it is not possible to remove the prefix, indicate this by writing ×.

REMEMBER: Use your dictionary to help you decide.

e.g. irregularity	regularity	irritant
miscellaneous		nongenarian
unhappiness		nonaligned
illegitimate		illustrious
miserable		impalpable
misapply		

Suffixes

Perhaps the most common suffix is –s, used to form the plural of most nouns in English. Because this is so common, dictionaries only include information on plurals where they are not formed by simply adding –s, or where there is an alternative.

EXERCISE 2.14

Look up the following nouns, and write down the plural form of each.

REMEMBER: When the dictionary gives no special indication, the plural suffix will be simply –s.

   Example: knife, knives   drug, drugs

foot	formula	matrix
mother-in-law	set-back	bacillus
criterion	diagnosis	cylinder
tomato		

Another common suffix to form the past tense and past participle of many verbs is -ed.

Example: I want that now.
I want**ed** that yesterday.
I have want**ed** that for a very long time.

Because this is usually a very simple matter of adding -ed, the dictionary only gives the past tense and the past participle forms when they are not made simply by adding -ed.

REMEMBER: this is only true when the dictionary is dealing with verbs.

Where adding -ed creates an adjective, this is included in the dictionary.

Example: advance (*vi,vt*); advanced (*part adj*).

Verbs

EXERCISE 2.15

Look up the following verbs, and write down the past tense and past participle of each.

REMEMBER: Where the dictionary gives no special information, the past tense and past participle are formed with the addition of the suffix -ed.

Verb	Past Tense	Past Participle		
e.g. write	wrote	written		
draw		distinguish		wring
beat		saw		happen
forecast				

To help you with **irregular verbs**, the dictionary also lists them in an appendix. Write down the page numbers where the list of irregular verbs can be found.

EXERCISE 2.16

A puzzle

How many words can you make from the letters that occur in the word 'haematology'?
The record so far is 114 words. Can you beat that?

PART 4

Using the Dictionary's Grammatical Information

Changes in Parts of Speech

We have already dealt with the abbreviations the dictionary uses to describe what part of speech a word is, and we have noted that a word may be a different part of speech in different contexts. Look back at Exercises 2.4 and 2.5 to refresh your memory of this.

Another way in which a word may act as a different part of speech is through the addition of a suffix. Some suffixes actually change the part of speech of a word: the original meaning is kept, but the 'new' word can be used in a different way in a sentence.

Example: The noun 'happiness' is *derived* from the adjective 'happy'.

We can also say:

The noun 'happiness' is a *derivative* of the adjective 'happy'.

EXERCISE 2.17

For each of the following sentences, find the *derivative* of the word, and write it down. To do this, you will need
- to decide what part of speech is appropriate for that place in the sentence;
- to look first at the headword in the dictionary, and then at the following headwords.

    e.g. **administer**
    The *administration* of a college is not easy.   (n)
    The office deals with *administrative* matters.   (adj)

1 **dim**
    The room was very ＿＿＿＿＿＿＿＿ lit.
    Through the ＿＿＿＿＿＿＿＿ I could just see the door.

2 **finance**
    The company is in ＿＿＿＿＿＿＿＿ difficulties.
    The bank asked if I was ＿＿＿＿＿＿＿＿ solvent.

3 **economy**
    We must be more ＿＿＿＿＿＿＿＿ if we are to save money.
    The ＿＿＿＿＿＿＿＿ situation is very worrying.

4 **pass**
   There was a _____ left between the boxes.
   He gave the article only a _____ glance.

5 **understand**
   His speech was so slurred that he was barely _____.
   She's a good mother. She has great _____.

6 **intelligent**
   She has a formidable _____.
   The writing is so _____ that I have no idea what it says.

7 **extreme**
   In politics, he is rather an _____.
   He is _____ hard working.

8 **pleasant**
   I have always been _____ to her.
   She broke the ice with a few _____.

9 **straight**
   Go _____ ahead, then take the third turning.
   I think we should try to _____ out this room.

10 **decent**
   He didn't even have the _____ to answer.
   Office workers are expected to dress _____.

To do this last exercise well, you would have had to be able to use the appropriate part of speech in each sentence. This information is in the dictionary. However, because this exercise is quite complex, it would be a good idea to do more practice in identifying parts of speech.

EXERCISE 2.18

What is the part of speech of each *italicized* word in the following passage?

In[1] 1928 Sir Alexander Fleming noted that some common green *mould*[2] had *grown*[3] among *bacteria*[4] which had *previously*[5] been planted in a *culture*[6] plate. *As*[7] the mould grew, *it*[8] formed a liquid which destroyed the *nearby*[9] microbe colonies. Fleming tried his liquid out on other types of bacteria *and*[10] found *that*[11] some were *quickly*[12] dissolved, while others were left *unharmed*[13]. He *named*[14] the fluid 'penicillin', *unaware*[15] that his chance discovery was to have *tremendous*[16] consequences.

Fleming realized that *penicillin*[17] had great antiseptic qualities, but the active principle in the mould was *too*[18] unstable and difficult *to*[19] extract. For a time, the only practical purpose of penicillin was to separate the *different*[20] types of bacteria from each other.

Verbs

One of the most useful things the dictionary can do is to give information on which prepositions and adverbial particles go with which verb.

EXERCISE 2.19

In each of the following sentences the wrong adverbial particle or preposition has been used. Look up the verb in your dictionary, and correct the particle.

    Example: I was posted *at* Venezuela for a year.   (incorrect)
              I was posted *to* Venezuela for a year.   (correct)

 1 He will familiarize himself to the company's site.
 2 He will be presented of a gift by the group.
 3 He was convicted for three different offences.
 4 I am in sympathy of what the police have suggested.
 5 I am keen in biology.
 6 He knows quite a lot in running a business.
 7 The judge would only have sentenced him for a month.
 8 I have attached my photograph with the letter.
 9 The cases are presided on by the village elders.
10 It is divided in five portions.
11 They accused the man for murder.
12 It is advertised on the *Post-Courier*.
13 I am interested for the position.
14 She promised to care to the children.
15 Over-fishing could result with extinction of fish.

PART 5

Using the Stylistic Information in the Dictionary

There are some words in English which should only be used in certain situations. They are appropriate only in a particular context: in another context a different word should be used. The dictionary indicates where the use of a word is restricted in some way by the use of labels such as 'formal' or 'informal', 'poetical' or 'technical'.

EXERCISE 2.20

Use your dictionary to find out when the words given below could be used, and then write an alternative which could be used in any situation (the *neutral* alternative).

e.g. *Word*   *Use*   *Neutral alternative*
    heretofore   legal   until now

bow-wow	cobber	tarsal	beget
kick the bucket	clink (n)	OK	hereto
brolly	o'er		

EXERCISE 2.21

Use your dictionary to decide in what context the words in each of the groups should be used. The words have the same basic meaning, but are appropriate to different styles. Make sure you read the *whole* entry to find the meaning you are looking for!

    Write down the neutral words which are suitable for most situations. (Note: sometimes more than one will be neutral!)

    Example: fellow   guy   man   bloke   chap

'Man' is neutral. The rest are colloquial or informal.

1 book	pick up	pinch	apprehend	arrest
2 bird	lady	woman	missis	female

3 hilarious	funny	jocose	a scream	comic
4 toilet	loo	bathroom	bog	lav
5 fool	twit	clot	idiot	booby
6 prison	clink	lock-up	jug	penitentiary
7 kill	murder	bump off	do in	slay
8 alcohol	spirits	hooch	drink	booze
9 girl	lass	chick	skirt	maid
10 friend	pal	companion	mate	buddy

EXERCISE 2.22

Look at the following sentences and phrases. Are the *italicized* phrases correct? Look up each entry in the dictionary and check.

REMEMBER: If the dictionary doesn't say you *can* write it, then *don't* write it!

   If you follow this simple rule, you can guarantee that what you say or write will always be correct.

1 I *egressed from* the room.
2 He *tiffed with* his wife last night.
3 We went for *a saunter*.
4 I *maligned him*.
5 The painter *hued* the clouds with red.
6 *To hull* peas.
7 He *totted* the bill.
8 His *wealthiness* is famous.
9 There were lots of *informations*.
10 He was a *youthly* looking man.
11 He *zeroed* the clock.
12 The *monthly* was delivered to the house.

UNIT 3

Library Skills

This unit will help you make good use of what is perhaps the most important academic facility in any educational institution—the library.

Around the world several systems of cataloguing materials are used by libraries: you should find out which system your library uses, and learn how books and journals are catalogued. Do this as soon as possible, for until you understand your own library's cataloguing system, it will be impossible to find the materials you are looking for.

Because there are several cataloguing systems, this unit can only give you very broad guidelines on how to use the catalogue and how to understand the call numbers of individual books. That does not mean that you should not try to understand them yourself; your tutor or the librarians themselves should help you.

Before you really get to know the catalogue, however, there are other things that you need to know about your library. Try to answer the following questions to help you get to know your library properly.

EXERCISE 3.1

1 What hours is the library open during weekdays?
2 When is it open at the weekend?
3 Is the catalogue on cards or on microfiche?
4 Is there a special reserve section?
5 If there is a special reserve section, why are books put in it?
6 If there is a special reserve section, for how long can you borrow a book from it?
7 How many books can you borrow at a time from the main collection?
8 Can you borrow books from the reference section?
9 Does your library have more than one level? If it does, what parts of the library are on each floor?
10 How long can books be borrowed for?

Now that you have some idea of the library in general, you can begin to look at what is in it.

PART 1

Understanding the Front Pages of Books and Journals

The information placed on the first one or two pages of every book is important for anyone wanting to find the book in the library, or to quote the source of a fact or an idea correctly. So if you want to find a particular book in your library, you will need to know **how to read the front page of a book**.

If you open any book at the first pages, you will see something like those on p. 38.

On the first page (the title-page) is the **title** of the book and the **author's name**. Pay special attention to how the name appears. You will have to use it exactly as it appears in the front of the book. If you are looking for this book in the library catalogue and you search for 'I. C. Ward' or even 'Ida Ward' you may well have difficulties finding it. Always use the name *exactly* as the author uses it on the title-page.

At the bottom of the title-page you can see the name of the **publisher** of the book, and the **place** where it was published. Sometimes this information does not appear on the first page, but only appears on the second.

The second page (the imprint page) has a symbol © followed by a name and a date. The symbol means 'copyright'—this need not concern you here. Below that comes information you will need to pay special attention to. You will see these words:

Published
Edition
Reprinted

To understand these words, it is necessary to understand how a book is produced. A book in a bookshop or on the shelves of a library has been through several stages after the author has written it. The author will have submitted a *manuscript* (usually typed pages) to a **publisher** who decides whether it is suitable for selling as a book. Once the publisher decides that it is, plans are made for how the book will look: how big it will be, what type of print it will have, and what colour the cover will be. Changes may be suggested to the author, or whole chapters may even be deleted if they are unsuitable. Once all this has been done the manuscript is sent to a **typesetter**; and proofs are checked by the author and editor. The final version of the book is sent to the **printer**, who prints each page, and binds the pages together between covers. The book is then ready to be sold.

THE PHONETICS OF ENGLISH

BY

IDA C. WARD

CAMBRIDGE

W. HEFFER & SONS LTD

First published .. *1929*
Second Edition .. *1931*
Third Edition (entirely revised, with additional chapters) 1939
Fourth Edition .. *1945*
Reprinted with minor corrections .. *1948*
Reprinted *1950*
Reprinted *1952*
Reprinted *1956*
Reprinted *1958*
Reprinted *1960*
Reprinted *1962*

Printed in Great Britain at the Works of
W. HEFFER & SONS LTD., CAMBRIDGE, ENGLAND

A popular book may be reprinted many times. Once the original books that the printer has made are sold, the publisher may ask him to print more. This is called a **reprint**. Each printing may sometimes be called an **impression**.

Perhaps after a few years if the book is still popular, the publisher may decide to add new information from the author or to update technical or other information, or to change the format of the book by changing the style of print or perhaps the size of the page. The new book that then appears is called a **new edition**. The first time the book is published, it is called a *First Edition* of the book. If the format changes, or information within the book alters, then the new book is called a *Second Edition*. Remember, the book itself will be substantially the same: it is merely the physical appearance that may have changed, and alterations to the text may range from minor revisions to major additions or revisions. A standard religious text like, for instance, *The Bible* or *The Koran*, may well have gone through hundreds, if not thousands, of different editions since they were first published, even though the text itself may have barely changed over the years.

In your academic work you will need to know which edition you are using. There are two reasons for this. The first is that often you will be looking for a book in the library because you have been referred to certain pages in a particular edition of it. The second reason is because you may want to quote from the book yourself, and to do this you will have to give the correct information about page numbers. The edition is important in both these instances because page numbers often change from edition to edition, or even whole chapters may have been inserted or removed. So if a writer wants to quote something on page 67 of his copy of Ida C. Ward's book, which happens to be the fourth edition, then he must tell his reader that it *is* the fourth edition. If the writer does not do this, then someone reading his work who has, say, the third edition, will look on page 67 and find something totally different. It is quite possible that any quotation chosen from the book will be on different pages in each of the four editions!

So, to identify the very book you are working from, you must know:

1 The edition—luckily this is easy: it must be the latest edition quoted on the second page! Identify the edition by giving its *date* of publication.
2 The place of publication—the country is usually sufficient.
3 The publisher—different publishers may have published the same book over the years (think of *The Bible* or *The Koran* again).

REMEMBER: You need to give information on the publisher, *not the printer*. (You will rarely, if ever, need to provide information on the printing of a publication.)

If you look back at the example quoted at the beginning of this discussion you will see that the following information is necessary to identify the book correctly:

1 Author: Ida C. Ward.
2 Date of the actual edition being used: 1945.
3 Title: *The Phonetics of English.*
4 The place where the book was published: England.
5 The name of the publisher: W. Heffer.

This is quite a complicated example, as the book has gone through several editions and many reprints. Luckily most of the books you will be using will have had only one edition, and so you will need to quote only the last date of *publication* (but not the last date of *printing*, remember!).

This may sound pretty difficult, but in fact it is quite simple, provided you always remember to check all the information about the book: there are *five* pieces of information you must have.

Your next step is to find out **how to read the front page of an academic journal**.

Apart from the actual books in a library, there is also a section containing journals, or periodicals. Current issues of academic periodicals are usually displayed in a special section called the periodicals or journals section. Back issues are usually kept in the main part of the library, in bound sets. To find a particular issue of a journal, it is necessary to know how they are identified.

Journals play an important part in academic life, for it is in journals that most academics report the results of their research or try out new ideas in their particular field. Academic journals are usually linked specifically to one particular subject, and normally appear on a regular basis, perhaps three or four times a year. The journals are necessary in academic life, because they provide the means for academics to publish material that is not suitable to be converted into complete books—usually because what the academic has to say is too short.

The value for journals to students and to academics alike is that they provide a good source of ideas, and they present up-to-date information on current research in a given field.

Look at the front pages of this journal on pp. 42–3.

Apart from the title of the journal, there are several items of information that you need when looking for a particular source.

Usually you will have been given the title of an article by your tutor, or you will have come across the name of the article in another of your readings. To find the particular article you are looking for, you will need to know much more than the title of the journal and the article. This is because, unlike books which are (usually) published only once, journals appear regularly, sometimes as frequently as once a month. Most academic journals appear four times a year, but this is by no means an inflexible rule.

Because journals appear so frequently, it is not enough to simply rely on the year of publication to identify a given issue. For this reason journals give a **volume number** and an **issue number** on their front cover. The volume number is usually connected with the year: thus Volume I (or 1) of a given journal will be the first year that the journal appeared. Volume VI (or 6) will be the sixth year it appeared, and so on.

The issue number tells the reader which issue within the year the journal is. So if a particular journal has 'Vol. IV (3)' on the front cover, it tells the reader that it is the third issue of the journal in the fourth year of the journal's life. Without the issue number, anyone looking for a particular article would have to wade through all the issues of that journal for a given year—which in some cases could amount to several thousand pages!

So to identify a particular article in a journal you need to have the following information, apart from the author's name:

- the title of the article;
- the volume number;
- the issue number;
- the page on which the article begins.

In the case of the journal shown below, you would need to supply the following information if you are to fully identify, say, the third article:

1 The author's name: Cynthia White.
2 The date of publication: 1989.
3 The title of the journal: *ELT Journal*.
4 The title of the article: 'Negotiating communicative language learning in a traditional setting'.
5 The volume number: 43.
6 The issue number: 3.
7 The pages on which the article occurs: p. 213.

As we shall see later on, there are very strict conventions about how you write out this information, but for the time being it is only necessary to bear in mind that there are *seven* pieces of information needed to correctly identify an article in a journal.

All this information both about books and about journals is important, not only for finding references that you may have been given by your tutor but it is also necessary when you compile a *bibliography* at the end of an essay or paper. (You will see later, in Unit 7: Quoting Skills, how to put together a bibliography).

VOLUME 43/3
JULY 1989

An international journal for
teachers of English to speakers
of other languages

Oxford University Press
in association with
The British Council
and with IATEFL

ELT JOURNAL

Contents

ELT Journal   Volume 43   Number 3   July 1989

PART 2

Finding Sources in a Library

The Catalogue

There are two ways of finding materials for assignments in the library: by browsing along the shelves, and by using the catalogue.

Most libraries divide their catalogue into three sections:

- author catalogue;
- title catalogue;
- subject catalogue.

Your tutor or the librarians will show you how to use the catalogue to find books. This short exercise will help you to practise using the entries in the catalogue. Later in the unit you will get the chance to practise using the last one of these, the subject catalogue.

EXERCISE 3.2

Whether your library uses cards or microfiche for its catalogue, each book will have an entry on its own. Write out the entries for the books specified *exactly* as you find them in the catalogue. Then answer the questions that follow.

a In the author catalogue, look up William Golding.

1 How many novels written by this author does your library have?

2 Choose *one* of the novels written by this author, and write out the catalogue entry, **exactly as you find it**. Don't forget to include:
- the call number;
- the author's name, exactly as it is written in the entry;
- the title in full,
- any further information that the catalogue entry may provide.

3 How many copies of this novel does your library have?

b Now look up the author H. Widdowson.

1 How many titles by this writer does your library have?

2 Choose *one* of H. Widdowson's books, and write out the catalogue entry, exactly as you find it.

3 How many copies of this book does your library have?

c 1 Now go to the subject catalogue and look up 'crocodiles'.
2 How many books does your library have on 'crocodiles'?
3 Choose one of the books listed, and write out the catalogue entry.
   How does this entry differ from the entry in the author section? Look up the entry for the title you have just chosen, and compare the two cards.
   Write out the entry for the book in the author catalogue, and note down any differences in the layout of the two cards.

d Now look up 'transport' in the subject catalogue. Choose one entry in this section and write out the catalogue entry.
1 How many entries did you find in the section concerned with 'transport'?
2 Did the section on 'transport' refer you to other types of transport? If so, what were they?

The Reference Section

Perhaps the most useful starting point in any search for sources is the reference section.

For this next exercise, you should go to the reference section. Don't go to the catalogue for this information; one of the aims of the exercise is to let you see what kinds of books the reference section contains: the best way of getting to know a library is to browse often through the shelves to see what is there!

EXERCISE 3.3

Look at the shelves in the reference section of your library. Does the library have books with the following titles?
Who's Who
A London telephone directory
A German/English dictionary
The Cambridge Encyclopaedia of Astronomy
The Book Publishers' Directory
Encyclopaedia Britannica
The Oxford English Dictionary
World Airways Guide
Butterworth's Medical Dictionary
Semiconductor Index
Official Rules of Sports and Games
The World of Learning
An Analytical Concordance of the Bible

There are of course many other books in the reference section, and you should not think that these are the only ones that you will ever need to refer to!

The next exercise will give you a chance to use some of the reference books on the shelves.

EXERCISE 3.4

From the list of topics below, choose *two* that are completely new to you, then spend half an hour in the reference section finding out as much as you can about the topics.

At the end of the time list the sources you have used: note the *name* of each book, its *publisher*, and the *date of publication*.

A special note: You may wish to begin with one of the encyclopaedias in your search for information. However, do not restrict your search to the encyclopaedias alone!

Ying and Yang	Voltaire	Boyle's law
Lung cancer	Batik	Albania
Tai Kwan Doh	Monetarism	Croquet
The Wallace Line	Japanese Kabuki	Frank Lloyd Wright
The silicon chip	Leonardo Da Vinci	

Choose only *two* of these.

EXERCISE 3.5

This is an exercise which gives you practice in looking for specific pieces of information.

Which reference books would you use to find out the following pieces of information? Write down your suggestions, and then check to see if you are right by looking for the information in the book itself.

1 The date when Ceylon changed its name to Sri Lanka.
2 The average annual rainfall in Singapore.
3 The name of the first president of the United States of America.
4 The names of the countries that are members of the European Economic Community.
5 The date of the discovery of penicillin.
6 The name of the man or men who first split the atom.
7 The name of the current Secretary of the United Nations.
8 The place where the last Olympic Games were held.
9 The names of the countries that are members of the British Commonwealth.
10 What the Victoria Cross is awarded for.
11 The place where the first heart transplant was performed.
12 The country which consumes the largest quantity of fish in the world.
13 What AIDS stands for.
14 The name of the longest river in the world.
15 The meaning of 'otorhinolaryngology'.

Assessing Sources

One danger with finding sources in a library is that not all sources are reliable! *It is very important to remember that just because something is written in a book, it isn't necessarily true!*

It is your responsibility to check that the sources you are finding are reliable and correct; that is why you should find more than one source for any fact, if at all possible!

Luckily, most tutors and lecturers will give you a lot of help in this area by suggesting sources that you may wish to follow up. However, you may find other material that looks useful for the assignment you are working on, and which you may wish to include. Before you do this, however, *beware!*

Before you make use of an article or book that you have found, *always* check the following:

1 **When was it written?** If it is more than five years old, it may well be out of date (but not necessarily so!).
2 **Who is the author?** Is he or she an authority in the field? You should look for information on the author either inside the front cover or on the back page if it is an entire book, or at the beginning or end of the text if it is an article in a journal. If the author is not someone with direct experience in the field, the text may well be misleading.
3 **Is the author biased in some way?** Has the author written the text from an extremist standpoint—religious, political or racial? If he or she has, the opinions and the conclusions the author comes to may well be unbalanced, and the author may have selected the facts to support the argument in such a way that the truth is distorted.
4 **What audience is the writer aiming at?** Is the text a serious academic piece, or something written for a more general audience? While references to articles and books written for general consumption may be perfectly acceptable in academic work, you should approach them with care. As a general, rule, avoid magazine and newspaper articles unless you have been specifically told to read them by your tutor or lecturer.

EXERCISE 3.6

Look at the following examples of articles that you may find in the books and journals in the library. What would make you doubtful about their usefulness to you as sources in an academic essay?

1 *Nuclear Energy: Recent Developments*, by Scott Walker, published by Barnes & Noble Ltd, 1955.
2 'Alluvial Pollution and Algal Mutation in the Ganges River Basin', an article by George Sprint, the well-known Australian sportsman and runner.
3 *The Case for Namibia: Justice for All*, a book by Pietr Botha (Prime Minister of S. Africa), published in Cape Town, 1982.
4 *English in Three Easy Lessons: Perfect English Straight Away*, by Professor B. J. Alcott, published by the Alcott Press, London, 1978.
5 *Earthquakes and God: The Necessary Connection*, by the Rev. Eli Brown, published by the Church Press, 1984.
6 *The USA's Imperialist Role in Nicaragua: An Impartial View*, by Dr C. Cosmovicz, published by the Roumanian Bureau of Information, 1985.
7 *The Role of the Jews in History*, by A. Hitler, 1942.

EXERCISE 3.7

You have been given a brief assignment called 'Limiting Population Growth', and have found the following texts in the library catalogue. Which ones would you choose to look at? Some will be clearly useful, some will not. Others might need to be looked at quickly because you cannot tell at this stage whether they will be useful or not. Decide whether each book is likely to be:

(a) useful,
(b) not useful,
(c) possible.

(These are some actual books in a library covering the topic of birth control.)

1 *About Conception and Contraception*
   (motion picture)
   12 mins, col., 16 mm, sound

2 Berelson, Bernard
   The Great Debate on Population Policy: An Instructive Entertainment
   New York, The Population Council, 1975

3 Billings, John
   The Ovulation Method: The Achievement or Avoidance of Pregnancy by a Technique Which Is Safe, Reliable and Morally Acceptable
   Melbourne, Advocate Press, 1972

4 *Biology of Fertility Control by Periodic Abstinence: Report of a WHO Scientific Group,*
   Geneva, WHO, 1967
   WHO Technical Report Series No. 360

5 *The Growth and Control of World Population*
   London, Weidenfeld and Nicolson, 1970

6 *Cross-cultural Comparisons: Data on 2 factors in fertility behaviour; report on a project of a sub-committee on comparative fertility analysis of the International Union for the Scientific Study of Population*
   Prepared by Ronald Freedman and Lolagene C. Coombs
   New York, The Population Council, 1974

7 Cuca, Robert
   Experiments in Family Planning: Lessons from the Developing World
   Baltimore, John Hopkins Press, 1977

8 Davis, Geoffrey
   Interception of Pregnancy: Post-conceptive Fertility Control—Emmenology Revisited
   Sydney, Angus & Robertson, 1984

9 Eckholm, Eric P.
   Health—the Family Planning Factor
   Washington: Worldwatch Institute
   Includes bibliographical references

10 *Family Planning Handbook for Doctors*
   Edited for the IPPF by Ronald L. Kleinmann
   London, International Planned Parenthood Federation

11 *Family Planning in Health Services*
   Report of WHO Expert Committee
   Geneva, WHO, 1979

12 *International Conference on Population Planning*
   Lahore, Pakistan, FPA of Pakistan, 1973

13 *The Relationship between Family Size and Maternal and Child Health*
    London, IPPF, 1970
    IPPF Working Paper No. 5

14 Levin, Harry L.
    The Use of Radio in Family Planning
    Oklahoma, World Neighbors Press, 1981

15 Maine, Deborah
    Family Planning: Its Impact on the Health of Women and Children
    Colombia University Press, 1981

16 Marshall, John
    Planning for a Family: An Atlas of Temperature Charts
    London, Faber, 1965, repr. 1973

17 Masere, Lesley J.
    The Fourth Child/Cartoon story
    POM Primary Health Training Centre, 1984

18 Pyle, Leo
    Pope and Pill
    London, Longman, 1968

19 Rubin, Alan
    Family Planning Today
    Philadelphia, Davis, 1969

20 Stopes, Marie Carmichael
    Contraception (Birth Control), its Theory, History and Practice: A Manual for the Medical and Legal Professions
    London, John Bale and Sons, 1926

If you had to limit yourself to looking at only three of these sources, which would you choose?

PART 3

Finding More About Your Topic, Using the Subject Catalogue

This section of the unit will concentrate on the subject catalogue, for it is perhaps the most difficult to use. It is worth taking the effort to master the subject catalogue; once you have mastered it, it will become, without doubt, one of your most valuable assets while you are a student.

Whether the library catalogue is on cards or on microfiche, the problems are still the same. What should you look up to obtain more information on the topic you are researching?

The most important thing to remember is that you should be prepared to look up more than one subject area in the catalogue. The exercise that follows will give you more practice in this.

EXERCISE 3.8

For each of the following topics, suggest at least *three* more general terms which might be worth investigating in the subject catalogue:

Hookworm	Water power	Crime prevention
Kerosene	Meteors	Rail freight
Police Force	Beer	Cyclones
Cardamom		

In most cases, once you start to investigate a topic your problem will be of having too much rather than too little material. You will never be able to read all that the library has available—nor should you try to. You must be selective about what you are going to spend your precious time on.

Remember to use the skills practised in the previous section of this unit—that of selection of materials by looking at
(a) when it was written;
(b) who the author was;
(c) whether it is likely that the author is biased in some way;
(d) the audience the writer was aiming at.

Most of these questions can be answered by looking at the catalogue card.

EXERCISE 3.9

Choose one of the topics in the Exercise 3.8. Go to the library, and use the subject catalogue to find out what books your library has on the topic of your choice. Write two lists:
1 Up to four books that look as if they may be suitable.
2 Up to four books that look as if they will not be suitable.
   On this second list, write your reason for rejecting each book.

REMEMBER: Look under *all* the subject headings you used for your topic in the last exercise.

   When you write down the names of the four books that may be suitable, make sure you write the *call number* for each one in exactly the same way as it is written in the catalogue. If you do this every time you find a book in the catalogue, you will be able to save a lot of time when you go to the shelves for the books!

REMEMBER: Include the author's name, and the title *in full.*

   Prepare your list as below:

TOPIC _____

_____

Suitable Books
Book No. 1
Author _____
Title _____

_____
Call No. _____
(etc.)

Unsuitable Books
Book No. 1
Author _____
Title _____

_____
Call No. _____
Reason for its rejection:

_____
(etc.)

_____

EXERCISE 3.10—Assignment

Now choose a topic from your own subject area, perhaps part of the next assignment for one of your courses. Go to the subject catalogue and do the same as you did for the last exercise. Find four books that look as if they may be useful, and list them, together with their call numbers. Then list four titles that may *not* be suitable. For each of the four rejects, give at least one reason why the book is not suitable.

UNIT 4

Reading Skills

PART 1

Scanning—or How Much Do You Have to Read?

Every serious student has the same problem: how to get through the vast amount of reading given for each course. You know by now that there is just not enough time available for you to sit down and read everything line by line, word by word. It takes too long. Instead it is necessary for you to acquire a technique that will allow you to cover whole pages of text without having to read every single word.

The technique has basically two parts:
1 efficient scanning;
2 recognizing the main points of a text.

This section practises the first of these. The next section will practise the second.

Efficient Scanning

When an efficient scanner approaches an article in a periodical or newspaper, he takes in only the key words and phrases which allow him to follow the general sense of the passage. Such words tend to be *content* words—nouns and verbs—rather than the grammatical words like articles and prepositions. To give you some idea as to how little actual grammar we need when we are reading something, look at the exercises that follow.

| **EXERCISE 4.1** |

The following extract is a complete newspaper story. Many of the words have been left out, yet the sense of the original is still retained. Try to answer the comprehension questions that follow the story.

11 Escape in Crash

ELEVEN _____ lucky _____   _____ scheduled _____
_____   _____ Wye __ Rambak, _____
landing _____ Maredy   _____ director _____
___ Wednesday. _____   _____ yesterday ____ investigator
_____ Cessna _____   _____ safety department ____
damaged _____   already _____ determine
_____ survived without   _____ .
_____ injury.

1 What crashed?
2 How many passengers were there?
3 Were they hurt?
4 Where were they going?

5 What did the Director of the Civil Aviation Authority say yesterday?
6 When is the investigator going?
7 Why?

EXERCISE 4.2

Now look at the text itself at the end of this section, and underline the words you think are absolutely necessary to convey the meaning of the piece.

What implication does this exercise have for your own reading?

The problem of understanding a short newspaper article like the one above may seem to be much less difficult than when you are dealing with a much longer, more complex article. However, reading a lengthy article quickly is just as simple. Several factors help you:

(a) You do not approach a piece of reading without having some knowledge of the subject, no matter how slight. Whenever you scan a text, you should be looking for things that you **don't** know. *Don't waste your time reading things that you know already!*

(b) You should have clearly in your mind the reason *why* you are reading the text.

(c) If you ask the initial question 'What do I expect to learn from this passage', you will have a very much clearer idea of what you are looking for.

Full text of the newspaper article:

11 Escape in Crash

ELEVEN passengers had a lucky escape when their light aircraft crashed on landing at a remote strip in Maredy on Wednesday. The plane, a Broadens Airways Cessna 206, was extensively damaged—but the eleven passengers, including the pilot, survived without a single serious injury.

The plane was on a scheduled flight from Wye to Rambak, where it crashed. Civil Aviation director Mr Steven Woods said yesterday an investigator from the air safety department had already flown into the area to determine the cause of the crash.

Using Key Words and Key Terms

Look through Part 2 of this unit (pages 58–66), and *as quickly as possible* try to answer the following questions:
1 How many exercises are there?
2 How many sections does it fall into?
3 What is Part 1 all about?

What you have just been asked to do is to **scan** the relevant part of the unit for specific information. You have done this without having to read every word. Instead you have approached the pages with a definite purpose, looking for certain visual signals—for instance, Question 1, 'How many exercises are there?' How do you recognize an exercise? What features do you look for?

> Write down the features you have selected. Note that none of the criteria you have chosen involve reading every word on the page to recognize it!

Hopefully this will show you that, when we want to find a particular piece of information, often the quickest way to find it is first to make some intelligent guesses as to *where* and *in what form* that piece of information is likely to be found, then to scan the page to locate it. We do not have to read every word because we know what we are looking for. One example of this type of scanning is when you run your eye down a list of exam results to find your own score: you know the form your own name will appear in because you have seen it many times before and you know roughly where it will come in the alphabetical list. Your eye moves quickly down the page until it focuses on a likely looking form, which you then read more closely to find out exactly what you want to know.

> This skill is part of our daily lives. What other occasions are there when you scan a page looking a particular thing? Write down several examples.
> In the case of the exam result, what word would you be looking for? Your name, of course. This is called the **key word**. Now what about the examples you have just given from other occasions when you scan a page? Write down the key word you be looking for in each example.

EXERCISE 4.3

Look at the following essay titles. If you use key words to help you go through your readings, then you can speed up your search for information.

REMEMBER: You are going to select the actual words in the titles that you need to look out for in the readings you find, or are told to look at by your tutor.

1 What is AIDS? Describe the symptoms.
   (List key word(s))

2 Outline Thailand's rice production in the last ten years.
(List key word(s))

3 Describe development on the Amazon river complex.
(List key word(s))

4 Compare the education system of the USA with that of your own country.
(List key word(s))

5 Briefly explain the system of import quotas in the USA and in Japan.
(List key word(s))

Key terms

There is one problem with key words, however. Sometimes we are not sure of the exact key word we are looking for. For instance, an example of this is when we are trying to find the date when a man was born or a process was discovered. In a situation like this, we cannot expect to have an exact date in our mind when we look for the key word: instead, we must look for a *type* of word rather than an exact word. The exact word we called the key word, the type of word we shall call the **key term**.

Here are some examples of how using key terms helps in scanning.

a If you want to find out who discovered the transistor, and you find an article all about transistors, then the key term you would be looking for would be the *name of a person*.

If when you scan the passage you find more than one person's name, then you will have to read carefully where the names occur to find out whether or not they are referring to the discoverer of the transistor.

b If you want to find out whether an article you have found deals with political problems in one country only or in several countries, the key terms you would be looking for would be the *names of countries*.

If you find more than one country name, then you can safely assume that the article will deal with more than one country. If you can see only one country's name, then it is probable that the article will only be talking about that country.

EXERCISE 4.4

What key term would you look for in the following situations?

1 You are looking for infant mortality rates in an article on children in the Third World.

2 You are looking for some information on the frequency of tropical storms in the South Pacific in an article you have found.

3 You are looking for some information on the first missionaries into an area of New Guinea.

4 You are looking for some information on imports of vehicles into Japan.

5 You are researching rainfall averages in the different centres of the United States.

Using Titles to Anticipate the Contents of a Reading Passage

Looking at the Title

Titles of books and of chapters in books are carefully chosen by their writers. Titles in most academic works are chosen to highlight the main point of whatever is being presented. The writer of a particular title will almost certainly have considered every word with the utmost care. You should treat the titles you come across with the same amount of care. If you do, you will find that the titles will be of great help to you in your reading.

Titles are there to guide you to the main point of the text.

Look at the title-page and the contents page from *Disease and History* by Frederick C. Cartwright on pp. 59–60.

First, let us consider the title itself. Look at the individual words. Do you know what they mean? If you are not absolutely certain, then look up the words in your dictionary. If you use your dictionary for nothing else in your reading, you *must* use it to help you to understand the words in the titles you meet.

Once you are sure of the dictionary meanings of the words, you must go to the next stage, which is to look at the whole phrase, and make sure you understand that.

Although we proved earlier with the newspaper story that grammatical words are not vital to your general understanding of a text, they are very important in the title. Grammatical words like 'and' or 'but' or 'why' can often show how the ideas in the text are related to each other.

In the case of *Disease and History* the two words are linked together with 'and', so the author is highlighting a **connection**. It is this connection between disease and history that his book is all about. This leads us to the question we must ask ourselves when we begin looking at the book: 'What *IS* the connection between disease and history?' If, after you have read the book, you cannot answer this question in a sentence or two, then you can be sure that you have not grasped the main point of the book.

Look at how the change in connection between 'disease' and 'history' changes the probable main point of the book: *History of Disease* would probably be concerned with how diseases developed over the centuries. It would be

Disease
and
History

by

Frederick F. Cartwright

in collaboration
with Michael D. Biddiss

Rupert Hart-Davis   London

Contents

concerned with disease alone and have little to do with history. The question you should probably have in your mind when you approach a book with this title is: 'What history has disease had?', or 'How has disease developed from early times until now?' The answer to these questions will contain the main point of the book.

Books are large pieces of writing. Fortunately they are usually broken up into chapters which have titles. These chapter titles must be treated in the same way as the book title, for they provide clues to the reader as to how the writer has broken up his book: each chapter will have a main point of its own, which can be discovered by looking carefully at the chapter title.

Look at the contents page from *Disease and History*. Look at chapter 2, 'The Black Death'. If you go through the same process as you did with the title of the whole book, you will

1 make sure you understand the individual words;
2 make sure you understand the phrase these words are used in;
3 formulate a question in terms of that phrase.

This chapter title has only one grammatical word—'The' at the beginning. 'The' is not usually used in front of the noun 'death' except in phrases like 'the death *of* my uncle'—but there is no 'of' here. The author has put 'the' into the title because 'the Black Death' was the name given to a particular disease that swept Europe in the fourteenth century. This information is given in any good dictionary for second language learners.

Look up 'the Black Death' in your dictionary and write out the meaning.

This should show you very clearly that, even though the individual words are quite well known to you, it is the *combination* of the words that you need to look at, particularly if they are used in a title in an unusual phrase such as this one.

The words in the title, their meanings and the way they are joined in a phrase are major clues supplied by the writer to help his readers find his main point. However, there is one other element that is just as important: **your own general knowledge**.

Look at chapter 3, 'The Mystery of Syphilis'. The dictionary will give a useful paraphrase of 'mystery' and an explanation of 'syphilis'. The word 'of' highlights the fact that the author is concerned with an aspect of syphilis that cannot be explained. He is definitely not going to spend all his time telling his reader what syphilis is. Thus the question that we can ask when we approach the chapter may well be 'What cannot be explained about syphilis?' In fact you can make a very good guess as to what the chapter will be about if you use your general knowledge about syphilis (or if you look up 'syphilis' in the dictionary). If you know something about syphilis, then that something cannot be a mystery! So the chapter cannot be about that.

Do you know how syphilis is passed on! Do you know what happens to people who get syphilis? Do you know the symptoms of syphilis? Probably you know the answers to all these questions: if you do, then none of them can be mysteries!

So what is left?

Do you know when syphilis started? Or where is started? Or how it started?

You certainly do not: in fact nobody knows any of these things for sure. These questions are all about the *origins* of syphilis and that is probably what a chapter entitled 'The Mystery of Syphilis' is going to be about.

You have used your general knowledge of the subject to decide what is definitely *not* a mystery, and so when you come to scan the chapter for the answer to the question 'What is there that we do not know about syphilis?' you will not need to waste your time on any pages dealing with symptoms, effects or transmission of this disease.

Look at chapter 4, 'General Napoleon and General Typhus'.

What could this chapter be about? You probably know, or your dictionary will tell you, that 'general' is a rank in the army; 'Napoleon' was a famous soldier; 'and' indicates a connection between the famous general and another one whom you haven't heard of, and the dictionary doesn't recognize either (typhus is only described as an infectious disease). However, as this is a book about disease, the meaning of 'typhus' must be appropriate.

So, what is the connection between a famous general and a disease? That is what you have to find out from the chapter. Your general knowledge will help you here too: the author has connected two generals—so in all likelihood one defeated the other. Is Napoleon still alive? Maybe you know, maybe you don't. The answer doesn't really matter, for you do know that typhoid is still regarded as a serious threat to mankind. Therefore you can predict that, in the 'battle' between the two generals, it was Napoleon who was defeated.

By using your general knowledge, you can gain a good idea of what the chapter is probably about: how typhoid brought about the defeat of Napoleon.

Try this technique on the other chapters. Follow these steps with each one:
1 Look up the words to make sure you are absolutely sure about their meaning.
2 Make sure you understand the phrase the words are used in.
3 Formulate a question in terms of the meaning of the title as you now understand it, using your general knowledge of the subject to help you.

REMEMBER: This is a book about disease and history, and each chapter will be concerned with some aspect of disease; if your questions are not to do with disease, then you are probably on the wrong track!

Write down your questions regarding the meaning of the following chapter titles:
   Chapter 5, 'The Impact of Infectious Diseases';
   Chapter 6, 'Disease and the Exploration of Africa';
   Chapter 7, 'Queen Victoria and the Fall of the Russian Monarchy';
   Chapter 8, 'Mass Suggestion';
   Chapter 9, 'Man-made Problems Present and Future'.

Of course, at the moment you cannot get the factual answers to any of these because you do not have the book in front of you. However, it is important to note that you do not have to have the text in front of to show you that you must think both *before* and *after* reading a particular text to check that you have understood it.

EXERCISE 4.5

Look at the contents page of *How Much Are Public Servants Worth?* by J. Gretton and A. Harrison (p. 64), and look at Parts 1 and 2. Notice that these have chapters as sub-sections.

What questions can you ask yourself before reading that will help you to understand the main points of these chapters? You will have to ask questions first about the titles of each part, and then of the sub-sections.

Contents

EXERCISE 4.6

Look at the contents page of *Work, Unemployment and the New Technology* by Colin Gill (p. 66).

Look at the chapter called 'Introduction'. What are you going to ask yourself to ensure you look for the main points of this chapter?

Contents

PART 3

Finding Out the Content of a Text by Looking at the First Sentence of Each Paragraph

Once you have found a chapter in a book or an article in a journal that seems useful, you don't want to read the whole thing to find one or two items you need. It is better to look quickly through the entire text to get a good idea of what it is all about so that you can go straight to the section that seems most useful.

The easiest way of doing this is to **look at the first sentence of each paragraph**. Luckily most writers of English state the topic of each of their paragraphs in the first sentence. So just by reading each first sentence you will usually be able to find out what the text is about.

Let us look at an example. Imagine you have to write an essay on 'The Diet of Early Man', and you have found an article called 'Of Rice and Men' in the July 1986 issue of *Geographical Magazine*. You need to find out quickly if it covers anything that you do not know about, so you scan the passage, reading the first sentence of each paragraph *only*.

The full text of the article follows on p. 68.

Below is a list of the first sentences of each paragraph only of the text. If you read only these, this is what you will read:

The adoption of agriculture is perhaps the single most important change in the history of mankind over the last ten thousand years, not so much for its immediate impact as for its profound potential.

Much research has been devoted to the place, time and reason for the beginnings of wheat and barley cultivation in the Near East, and the initial steps towards the harvesting of maize of Central America.

Rice is known to have been cultivated in India by the fourth millenium BC, for example, but for the vast region which comprises mainland South East Asia, where wild rice flourishes to this day, there was, until recently, no information.

This was not for want of effort.

In the uppermost layers of Banyan Valley cave, he found some rice husks.

Sadly, Gorman's premature death brought his programme of fieldwork to a close but his quest was taken up again with the discovery of a site, Khok Phanom Di, in central Thailand in 1979.

OF RICE AND MEN

by Charles Higham and Bernard Maloney

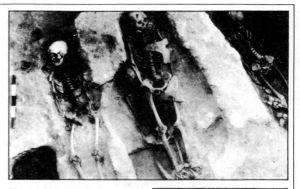

THE adoption of agriculture is perhaps the single most important change in the history of mankind over the last ten thousand years, not so much for its immediate impact as for its profound potential.

Much research has been devoted to the place, time and reason for the beginnings of wheat and barley cultivation in the Near East, and the initial steps towards the harvesting of maize in Central America. The archaeological record for early rice agriculture, however, is almost blank.

Rice is known to have been cultivated in India by the fourth millenium BC, for example, but for the vast region which comprises mainland South East Asia, where wild rice flourishes to this day, there was, until recently, no information.

This was not for want of effort. In 1972, Chester Gorman tested a well-known hypothesis of American geographer Carl Sauer, that agriculture commenced in South East Asia not by the cropping of cereals but of roots and fruit trees. Gorman's research took him to the rugged karst uplands of the Thai-Burmese border.

In the uppermost layers of Banyan Valley Cave, he found some rice husks. These caused great excitement because it was anticipated that they might date from as early as 6000 BC. But events were to prove otherwise. The radiocarbon dates indicated occupation in the first millenium AD for the layers in question and the rice was diagnosed as wild.

Sadly, Gorman's premature death brought his programme of fieldwork to a close but his quest was taken up again with the discovery of a site, Khok Phanom Di, in central Thailand in 1979. Two Thai archaeologists made significant finds here — not least, human burials — in 1979 and again in 1982, and our own fieldwork in the area has since uncovered a wealth of evidence of former occupation and, notably, fragments of rice chaff.

The site covers about five hectares 22 kilometres from the coast in an area known as Sundaland — a great drowned peneplain which, during the Pleistocene, connected the islands of South East Asia to the mainland. Despite its distance from the coast, the site is covered with shells of marine origin, indicating a much higher sea level than at present.

Early assessment showed the enormous value of the site in its potential for revealing the way of life of the people of Khok Phanom Di and how they exploited their environment. And it clearly raised the question: would we find evidence of early rice culture?

With the help of The Ford Foundation and Shell Thailand who provided funds, and researchers lent by the Thai Fine Arts Department and the Earthwatch Corporation of America, excavations were able to start in December 1984. Seven months later, we were seven metres down, at the bottom of the site.

Our early assessments of the layers of occupation indicated that Khok Phanom Di was inhabited for a considerable period of time. The site revealed itself as comprising three stratigraphic units, which we can call A, B and C. Our earliest findings in Zone A suggest that the site was first occupied about 4000 BC and that the transition to Zone B occurred 1500 years later. Khok Phanom Di would seem to have been located on a coastal spit or river mouth barrier. A sample taken from the soil immediately underlying the earliest archaeological deposits contains small to microscopic pieces of charcoal, indicating disturbance to the vegetation by fire before human occupation began.

It is likely that fairly substantial trees grew on the mound and that it had mangrove swamp on the seaward side. The presence of freshwater ponds is indicated by cores which revealed freshwater sediments, and by tiny molluscs found in the area. Access to mangrove swamps would not only have yielded a plentiful marine food supply but also wood which, judging by clay pots and thick layers of ash found on the site, was much in demand for firing pottery as well as for cooking fires. The presence of all these elements must have made Khok Phanom Di particularly attractive. In addition, there is likely to have been an abundant harvest of wild rice and possibly millets growing in the slightly brackish to fresh water.

The origins of rice culture in South East Asia are still obscure but the Khok Phanom Di archaeological site in central Thailand has yielded up fragments of rice chaff along with numerous human burials

The difficulty with tracking down evidence of rice cultivation is that the plant is self-pollinating and, therefore, does not shed much pollen to the wind for transporation. It is also impossible, using light microscopy, to distinguish its pollen from many other wild grass pollens. However, water transport of rice pollen is likely to be predominant around Khok Phanom Di. Certainly, we gained hope from some pollen and phytoliths which could be from rice, discovered in the upper part of the stratigraphic record. Food remains found at the site revealed a history of hunting, gathering and fishing along the mangrove-fringed beach. We found remnants of crabs, turtles, fish and shellfish, and, about 50 centimetres from the bottom of the site, the first fragments of rice chaff appeared.

Examination of the bones found on the site will also reveal something of the quality of the people's diet. Given the richness of the food remains found so far, it is unlikely that it was a poor one. However, 60 per cent of the burials discovered in Zone A were of very young infants.

THE layers of Zone B appear to cover a period when occupation ceased and the area was reserved solely for burials. Several more human remains were found here, one of which was in a large, deep grave that was particularly rich, with shell jewellery and lustrous black pottery incised with complex designs. Two of the other burials in this zone contained the remarkable remains of a dead person's stomach contents still in place. Surrounding layers also yielded remains of faeces which we are confident will turn out to be human. Studying them through a hand lens, we could see tiny fish bones and, on at least one occasion, a fragment of what looked like rice chaff. At the same time, faunal remains continued to be dominated by bones of fish and turtle, and claws of crabs.

The picture that emerges at present from Khok Phanom Di is that early settlements here, naturally, only lasted as long as the local environment could sustain them. As population increased in the area, the limited number of rich estuarine enclaves could no longer accommodate them. They began to move further into the harsher environment of the interior plains of South East Asia where the long dry season made food storage necessary. They chose to live where tributary streams provided gentle but predictable flooding in the rainy season, and cleared the flood plains for rice plots.

The story of early rice cultivation in South East Asia is still unclear. But the critical role of Khok Phanom Di is that the sedentary community there, and others like them, no doubt, along the region's whole coast, were the mainspring for the settlement of the interior by people familiar with harvesting of rice. Testing our hypothesis over the next few years may prove to be as exciting as those seven months spent excavating Khok Phanom Di.

Charles Higham is professor of anthropology at the University of Otago, New Zealand. Dr Bernard Maloney is lecturer in geography at The Queen's University, Belfast

The site covers about five hectares 22 kilometres from the coast in an area known as Sundaland . . .

Early assessment showed the enormous value of the site in its potential for revealing the way of life of the people of Khok Phanom Di and how they exploited their environment.

With the help of the Ford Foundation and Shell Thailand who provided funds, and researchers lent by the Thai Fine Arts Department and the Earthwatch Corporation of America, excavations were able to start in December 1984.

Our early assessments of the layers of occupation indicated that Khok Phanom Di was inhabited for a considerable period of time.

It is likely that fairly substantial trees grew on the mound and that it had mangrove swamp on the seaward side.

The difficulty with tracking down evidence of rice cultivation is that the plant is self-pollinating and therefore does not shed much pollen to the wind for transportation.

Examination of the bones found on the site will reveal something of the quality of people's diet.

The layers of zone B appear to cover a period when occupation ceased and the area was reserved solely for burials.

The picture that emerges at present from Khok Phanom Di is that early settlements here, naturally, only lasted as long as the local environment could sustain them.

The story of early rice cultivation in South East Asia is still unclear.

If you read these sentences quickly one after another, you will have a very clear idea indeed as the main points in the text.

Now check whether you have really understood the main points: try to sum up the content of the passage *in one sentence*, using your own words.

GOLDEN RULE

If you can't sum up what you've read by explaining it briefly in your own way, then you haven't really understood it!

EXERCISE 4.7

Another text follows for you to practice on.
- Look at the first sentences only.
- Try to sum up what they contain by limiting yourself to one sentence, using your own words.

Now select one of the readings for your next assignment in one of your major subjects, and do the same thing.

We will be practising this again in the Unit 5: Notetaking Skills.

30   New Scientist 22 January 1987

TECHNOLOGY

Ballooning for a place in the sun

Mary Fagan

Up, up and away on hot air and hope?

A SOLAR-POWERED hot-air balloon will attempt this summer to fly across the Atlantic. To succeed, it will have to break three times over the existing time and distance records for hot-air balloons.

The attempt is to be made by Richard Branson, of Virgin, and Per Linstrand, a designer with the British balloon manufacturer Thunder and Colt. last year Branson broke the record for a marine crossing of the ocean in Virgin Atlantic Challenger, a power boat.

Until now, hot-air balloons have been unable to carry enough fuel to go further than around 1500 kilometres—the endurance record is less than 28 hours. Branson hopes to make his crossing by relying mainly on heat from the sun.

The key to the attempt is a fabric, developed by ICI for the flight, that will allow more infrared radiation from the sun into Virgin Atlantic's balloon to maintain its heat. It will also allow less heat to escape than from conventional fabrics.

Flying in June, when daylength is longest, the balloon will travel at between 25 000 and 30 000 feet. The sun should power the balloon for 18 hours a day.

ICI will make the fabric from "rip-stop" balloon nylon and polyurethane film laminated together. The nonporous polyurethane will help to prevent air and heat from leaking out, while the nylon is woven in a way which inhibits tearing. It will be dark-coloured on the outside to help to absorb energy from the sun, and with a reflective aluminium coating on the inside. Four propane gas burners will be needed for take-off, but only one will top up the sun's energy during flight.

The Virgin balloon will be twice the size of the biggest hot-air balloon to date—59 metres high and broader than a jumbo jet—and will be able to carry 12·5 tonnes.

Virgin's other novel plan is the use of a pressurised capsule similar to those used in space flight. Without it, the crew could not endure the very low temperatures and oxygen levels at high altitudes. The crew will also use the "low-residue" diet developed by NASA for the Apollo mission to avoid the need to defecate.

Branson plans to fly the balloon from New York to London over three days in June. It will drop from its ceiling of about 30 000 to 25 000 feet as the sun goes down at night. He and Linstrand aim to ride the jet stream that at these altitudes flows across the Atlantic from west to east at an average speed to 50 knots.

They acknowledge that their main fear is unexpected thunderstorms that could rip the balloon to pieces.

Robin Batchelor, who taught Branson to fly, thinks there is a chance the sun could be too hot during the middle of the day. Unless the crew use a "dump panel" in the balloon to release some hot air, he says they could go up to "incredible" heights. The existing altitude record for a hot air balloon is just below 56 000 feet. To win a place in the record books a crew normally has only to maintain an altitude for around 10 minutes. But Batchelor points out that no one knows how a balloon will respond to the very strong sunlight and cold temperatures at such heights for longer periods of time.

Should the balloon burst in a storm, the capsule can be detached using explosive bolts. It is equipped with parachutes to allow it to descend to Earth. □

Custom built burners capable of operating at heights of up to 50 000 ft

Emergency parachute

Explosive bolts permit quick release of envelope

Remote control TV cameras

Observation dome and escape hatch

Liferaft

Emergency parachute

Satellite dish for live TV coverage

Entrance hatch

Storage

Fuel cylinder cells

Custom built sleeper seats

Temperatures in the capsule are unlikely to be much above freezing point during the flight

Problems ahead for the television hype

SUCCESS for the flight will depend as much on good communications as on new materials and favourable winds. Sponsor Cellnet has already advised Virgin to seek expert help from British Telecom on setting up its mission control.

"They know what they want but not how to achieve it," says Brian McPhee, marketing manager of Cellnet.

Richard Branson stands little chance of achieving his aim of sending live satellite television pictures back to Britain from the balloon. The problem lies with the satellite dish needed to transmit the signals. Chris Moss, Virgin's project officer, says: "We will use three video cameras inside the capsule and two outside. The balloon envelope is so big that we can put a large satellite trans-mitter and receiver dish inside."

The snag here is that the curved inner surface of the metallised layer of fabric could scatter the microwave signals back onto the dish.

The other problem is that having the dish inside could damage the balloon during inflation. Tom Barrow, project manager at Thunder and Colt, says: "The communications equipment will have to be outside the balloon."

Even if the dish can be mounted somewhere on the outside of the flight capsule, TV transmission will be difficult. The dish would need to be large and aligned with an accuracy of 1 degree. News crews on ships during the Falkland crisis found out how awkward it is to transmit TV pictures from a moving platform to a satellite for relay to Britain. They ended up sending ordinary television film reels by air.

A typical portable satellite system used by news crews is the Marconi Newhawk. It costs £125 000, weighs nearly 200 kilograms and relies on a dish with a diameter of 2·1 metres. This is a hefty weight for a long-distance balloon journey. Mike Garnett of Marconi says that the stabilisation problem at least could be solved by devising a gyro-stabilised system. "But that would need long, hard work," he said.

Branson's best bet could be to drop video-tapes by parachute or to ask British Telecom for advice on how to send still video pictures by conventional radio link.

Barry Fox

PART 4

Reading for an Essay

The next few exercises are based on a series of articles about the world's fisheries.

Do not look at the texts yet!

EXERCISE 4.8

Your purpose in reading the text is to research an assignment, 'Current Attempts to Farm Fish (Aquaculture) in South-east Asia'.

Before you can decide what key words and key terms you will be looking for, it is important for you *to establish what you know already*. There is no point looking for things you know already!

1 Write down three things that you know already about farming fish (not necessarily in South-east Asia).
2 Ask yourself 'What questions do I hope the article will answer?' These will relate directly to the topic of the assignment. They will be 'facts' you do not know—*not* the facts you have just written down. Write out the questions you can expect the article to answer. Then discuss your questions with a partner. Are your partner's questions reasonable? Is it reasonable to expect them to be found in the text?
3 As a result of what you have done so far, you can ask 'What key words and/or key terms will I be looking out for to help me?' ('Fish' or 'Fisheries' will not be one, as the whole series of articles is about that.) Remember to look at the essay title: you are researching *current* attempts, not past ones, and it is in South-east Asia, not the Pacific!
   Now:
a Scan the three articles, and decide which one will be most useful for this exercise.
b Look quickly through the relevant section, and try to find the answers to the questions you have written down. Remember, you may not find all the answers in these articles.
   This should take you no more than ten minutes.

EXERCISE 4.9

Your purpose in reading the texts is to research an assignment, 'The Size of Fish Catches in the Pacific Region'.

Follow the same pattern as in the previous exercise.
1 Your previous knowledge about the size of fish catches in the Pacific.
2 Questions you hope the articles will answer.
3 Key words/key terms to look for.

EXERCISE 4.10

Your purpose is to research an assignment, 'The Role of Japan in the Development of Southeast Asia's Fisheries'.

Follow the same procedures as in Exercises 4.7 and 4.8. This time work on your own, and try to do it all in five minutes!

Once you have completed these exercises, look at what you have written beside questions 1–3 in each section. They should be different for each part. Are they?

They should be different because, if you have approached the task correctly, you will have been using the texts for *three different purposes*.

If you are clear about *why* you are reading the text, you will 'read' articles of any length much more efficiently!

OVERVIEW

Under-paid, second-class citizens—that's fishermen

By Elizabeth Cheng in Hongkong

The level of fisheries development in Asia varies widely from country to country, depending on the quality of government planning and the availability of technological know-how. Most fishing communities in Asia live on the brink of starvation. They are largely ignored by their governments or are given low priority in national development plans.

While the 200 nmi national fishing zone, established in the 1970s, is widely recognised as a necessary step in conserving fishery resources and in helping coastal states (the majority of which are developing countries) improve their economies, fishing families have made little advance in their standard of living. Many of them have even failed to keep their status quo, having fallen victim to superior foreign fishing craft (often in joint ventures with the government) or are evicted to make way for urban development.

Singapore, the Philippines and India provide prime examples of how fishing communities have been uprooted to make way for, respectively, a new airport, housing estates and tourist resorts. In Malaysia, where government support for the fisheries sector is among the most comprehensive in the region, about half the fishing population lives below the poverty line — in stark contrast to the general standard of living in the country where per capita income is among the highest in Southeast Asia. The government's fisheries-development policies have been criticised for their inconsistency and, in some cases, for their partiality towards big-time fishing which has been blamed for wasteful and ecologically damaging use of resources.

In India, where there is no centrally planned fisheries-development programme, foreign-owned vessels are seldom supervised and are virtually free to fish at will and send their catch directly to their home markets. This has provoked a growing spate of protests (at times violent) by local fishermen who found their livelihood threatened. It is ironic that while India is the world's top supplier of shrimps and a major exporter of fish, most of its people are undernourished. India's average annual consumption per person of fish (often the only source of protein) is 3.7 kgs compared with some 40 kgs consumed in the developed world and about 20 kgs in many other developing countries.

Critics note that where foreign exchange is earned from the export of food, it is seldom used to buy low-cost nutritive food for the needy. Instead, it is used for the purchase of luxury goods. According to A. J. Vijayan, secretary of the National Fishermen's Forum of India

THE FISH CATCH IN THE ASIA-PACIFIC REGION

(tonnes '000) Country	1977	1978	1979	1980	1981	1982*	1981-82 (% change)
World Total	66,164	70,544	71,253	71,065	74,499	74,835	+0.5
Asia	19,025	18,891	18,492	18,667	19,724	19,755	+0.2
Bangladesh	835	640	646	646†	687	691	+0.6
Brunei	2	3	3	3†	3†	3†	—.
Burma	519	541	565	565†	595	584	−1.7
China	4,463	4,394	4,054	4,135	4,377†	4,377†	—
Hongkong	158	162	190	195	175	172	−1.5
India	2,312	2,306	2,343	2,305	2,415	2,400	−0.6
Indonesia	1,568	1,642	1,766	1,853	1,863	1,957	+5.0
Japan	10,123	10,184	9,966	10,398	10,657	10,657†	—
North Korea	1,190	1,260	1,330	1,330†	1,500†	1,550†	+3.3
South Korea	2,085	2,092	2,162	2,091	2,366	2,281	−3.6
Malaysia	619	685	696	737	764	679	−11.2
Maldives	26	26	28	34	35	35†	—
Pakistan	270	293	300	300	318	300	−5.6
Philippines	1,509	1,495	1,475	1,557	1,687	1,781	+5.6
Singapore	15	16	17	17†	16	16†	—
Sri Lanka	139	157	166	186	207	211	+2.2
Thailand	2,188	2,095	1,716	1,650	1,650	1,650†	—
Others	1,127	1,084	1,035	1,063	1,068	1,068	—
Oceania	66	106	98	96	117	117	—
Australia	128	123	127	120	130	161	+23.9
Cook Islands	1†	1	1	1†	1†	1†	—
Fiji	8	9	20	19	24	24†	—
New Zealand	83	100	110	117	108	112	+3.4
Papua New Guinea	26	53	30	30†	27	27†	—
Samoa	1	1	1	1†	3	3†	—
Solomon Islands	16	21	28	28†	27	27†	—
Tonga	1	1	2	2†	2†	2†	—
Others	13	20	16	15	32	32	—

* Preliminary data. †Food and Agriculture Organisation (FAO) estimate.
Source: FAO Yearbook of Fishery Statistics. (Latest figures available.)

(representative of fishermen's trade unions in the country), the introduction of purse-seiners has failed to increase the total highly valued sardine catch. Instead, it has resulted in a sudden decline in catch for the small fishermen. "Year after year, thousands of fishermen are thrown into dire poverty and unemployment," he said.

Vijayan charged that about 1.3 million tonnes of fish a year are wasted, having been sifted by foreign-owned trawlers fishing in Indian waters for high-quality varieties. In upgrading fishing technology, cost is often a major obstacle. The price of an outboard engine has jumped from Rs 6,000 (US$520) three years ago to Rs 12,000, said Vijayan, while spare parts are hard to get at affordable prices as a result of price manipulation by local sales agents.

The United Nations Food and Agriculture Organisation (FAO) observes that the world marine-fish catch, in volume terms, has not increased significantly since 1970, reflecting in part over-exploitation of resources. More damaging than over-fishing has been the waste of economic resources, which has hardly been checked by national implementation of a 200-mi restricted zone. Wastage has been estimated on a worldwide basis, to be in the region of 5 million tonnes.

The pattern of fish production has changed dramatically in the past decade with the introduction of extended jurisdiction. Joint ventures between governments and transnational companies have mushroomed while conglomerates which have had the run of the ocean now face numerous restrictions, resulting in a tendency to diversify into aquaculture to compensate for trimming of long-distance fishing. A case in point is Fiji, where the government earned virtually nothing from commercial exploitation by foreign vessels off its coast until the mid-1970s. The Fijian Government has since moved to rectify this situation and has set up a number of joint ventures with Japanese companies.

Despite an increase in the number of joint ventures in the Pacific islands and a concomitant rise in revenue to their governments, these countries continue to import fish — mostly canned — while exporting fresh fish. Nutritional expert George Kent, of the University of Hawaii, observes that poor countries tend to sacrifice domestic nutritional

JAPAN

Loans exceed sales of ¥3 trillion

By Hikaru Kerns in Tokyo

The Japanese fishing industry is burdened by heavy debt and faces dull growth in fish consumption, factors that threaten to force a shakeout of as much as 20% of the industry in coming years. Loans outstanding to the fishing industry as a whole exceed its annual sales. Many small and medium enterprises are struggling to avoid going deeper into debt but must borrow to cover operations and the government is encouraging a shrinkage of the number of enterprises in the industry so as to enable the survivors to make satisfactory profits.

The annual sales of the Japanese fishing industry in 1983 were about ¥3 trillion (US$12.4 billion), on a gross catch of about 11 million tonnes. Japan is the world's leading supplier of fish, followed by the Soviet Union which produces about 10 million tonnes. However, the Japanese catch has been virtually stagnant since 1972 when the 10 million-tonne level was reached. The past few years have been difficult. The sudden increase in fuel costs in 1979 forced most fishing enterprises to take out loans to cover operational expenses and needed capital investment, in the belief that better times were ahead. The industry has since come to rely on loans. Debt-servicing is estimated to be about ¥240 billion this year, still leaving loans outstanding of more than ¥4 trillion.

As one member of the Zengyoren, the cooperative representing 3,000 local fishing cooperative units, said: "The industry is working just to support the bank payments." Both government and private sources estimate that small and medium enterprises engaged in coastal fishing, mostly household units, do not break even; but due to income from other sources they are able to continue operations.

The Ministry of Agriculture, Forestry and Fisheries estimates that, as of March 1982, the agricultural and fisheries cooperative banking institutions, including Norinchukin Bank and Shingyoren, held about ¥1.6 trillion worth of loans to the fishing industry. Commercial banks held about ¥800 billion, while governmental banking institutions (mainly the Agriculture, Forestry and Fisheries Financing Corp.) were owed ¥500 billion. However, both government and private sources say that a massive default is unlikely because of industry-wide and governmental cooperation available to the debtors, including help in restructuring loans.

One of the major aggravations has been soaring fuel costs. Fuel now accounts for 23% of costs for coastal fishing, compared to 14% in 1978 and is now the biggest expense after depreciation which accounted for 24% of total expenditures. However, though wages to salaried fishermen are not far below the national standard for salaried workers — and for several years until recently

exceeded it — wages as a percentage of total expenditure have declined to 16% from 27% in 1970, reflecting the introduction of labour-saving equipment.

Besides the problems of heavy loan obligations and high fuel costs, the Japanese fishing industry has been forced, like other distant-water fishing enterprises in Asia, to increase its catch from nearby waters to compensate for the imposition of 200-mi territorial fishing zones by countries around the world. Distant-water fishing, which reached a peak of 4 million tonnes in 1974, has been reduced to 2 million. Coastal fishing, including aquaculture, has yielded a catch close to 3 million tonnes since the mid-1970s, but offshore fishing has increased from 4 million tonnes in 1974 to 6 million tonnes and made up for the diminished distant fishing zones.

But the species of fish available offshore and in coastal waters, such as sardine and cod, do not appeal to Japanese consumer tastes. As a result, while being the world's top producer, Japan is also the biggest importer of fish. Imports in fiscal year ended March 1983 totalled ¥1.05 trillion on a volume of 1.2 million tonnes, up from ¥879 billion in value and 1.1 million tonnes in volume during the previous year. At the same time, Japan exported 0.7 million tonnes worth ¥260 billion in fiscal 1982, mostly canned sardines, mackerel and tuna as well as fishmeal.

A problem is what to do with surplus sardines and mackerel. As recently as 1975, about half the sardine catch was used for human consumption, but in recent years production has far exceeded demand so that about three-quarters of the annual catch is now sold as fishmeal, feed for aquaculture or bait for fishing. Mackerel consumption has declined, but so has the annual catch. Currently, about one-third of the Japanese production of fish is accounted

Tuna in Tokyo: some sell at US$17,400 each.

requirements for foreign exchange.

A voracious consumer, Japan not only accounts for 15% of worldwide catch (at 11.3 million tonnes in 1983, it is the world's largest fishing country followed by the Soviet Union and China) but is also the world's largest net importer of fish at well over US$4 billion, more than half of that from Asian countries. Its fishermen and fishing companies, however, are mired in debts to financial institutions.

Studies show that the most valuable fish resources are found off the coasts of East and Southeast Asia. It is also in Asia that fish-farming is the most developed — the Asia-Pacific region produced 7.3 million tonnes in 1980, compared with total world output of 8.7 million. The FAO reported that total external loans for aquaculture projects in Asia more than tripled to US$52.8 million in 1981 from 1978 — and this trend appears to be continuing with the lending emphasis gradually swinging away from marine fishing.

Although many Asian countries are seriously looking into ways of improving their fisheries sector, not without substantial help from the FAO, their efforts centre almost exclusively on the development of fishing and fish-farming for export purposes, often to the detriment of local fishing communities. There are few government programmes to help these people acquire more competitive and self-sustaining skills and equipment. In the absence of adequate planning, displaced fishermen are likely to become a liability to their countries. ■

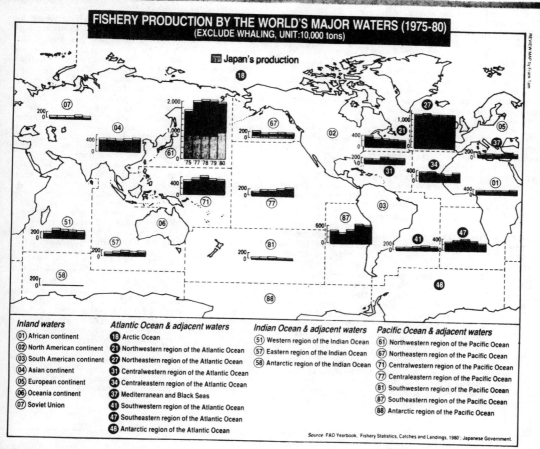

FISHERY PRODUCTION BY THE WORLD'S MAJOR WATERS (1975-80)

(EXCLUDE WHALING, UNIT:10,000 tons)

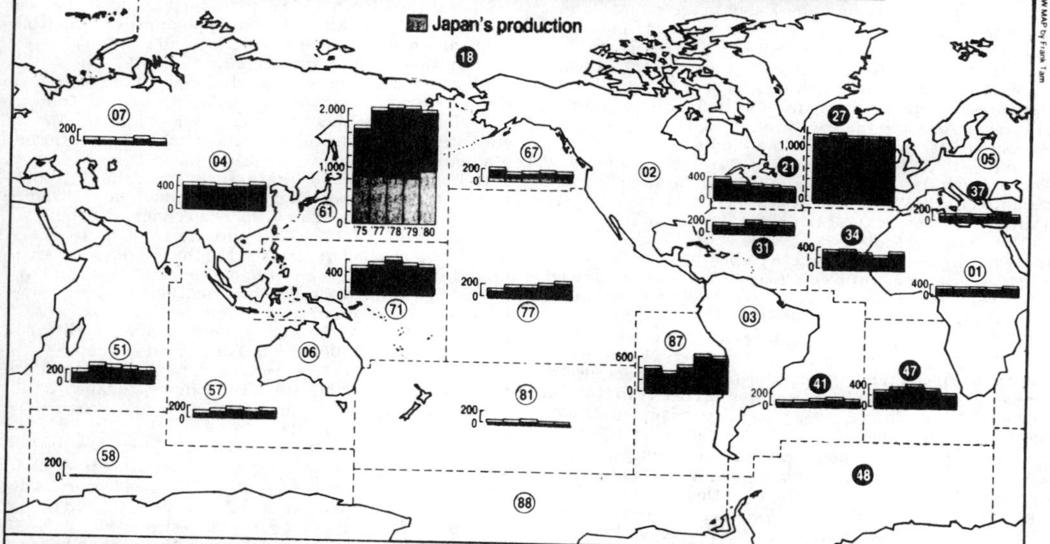

Inland waters
- (01) African continent
- (02) North American continent
- (03) South American continent
- (04) Asian continent
- (05) European continent
- (06) Oceania continent
- (07) Soviet Union

Atlantic Ocean & adjacent waters
- (18) Arctic Ocean
- (21) Northwestern region of the Atlantic Ocean
- (27) Northeastern region of the Atlantic Ocean
- (31) Centralwestern region of the Atlantic Ocean
- (34) Centraleastern region of the Atlantic Ocean
- (37) Mediterranean and Black Seas
- (41) Southwestern region of the Atlantic Ocean
- (47) Southeastern region of the Atlantic Ocean
- (48) Antarctic region of the Atlantic Ocean

Indian Ocean & adjacent waters
- (51) Western region of the Indian Ocean
- (57) Eastern region of the Indian Ocean
- (58) Antarctic region of the Indian Ocean

Pacific Ocean & adjacent waters
- (61) Northwestern region of the Pacific Ocean
- (67) Northeastern region of the Pacific Ocean
- (71) Centralwestern region of the Pacific Ocean
- (77) Centraleastern region of the Pacific Ocean
- (81) Southwestern region of the Pacific Ocean
- (87) Southeastern region of the Pacific Ocean
- (88) Antarctic region of the Pacific Ocean

Source: FAO Yearbook, Fishery Statistics, Catches and Landings, 1980'; Japanese Government.

for by sardine and the fishing industry has tried, with very small success, to persuade the public that eating sardines promotes health.

Prawns are Japan's biggest fish-import item. India and Indonesia each provide about ¥50 billion worth of prawns to Japan, while Australia, China and Thailand together provide another ¥75 billion worth. The United States is the source of most salmon and trout imports valued at about ¥75 billion, while South Korea and Taiwan provide about 80% of Japanese imports of tuna and marlin. Spain and South Korea are major suppliers of squid and octopus.

Japanese fish exports (which includes pearls) go mainly to the US, which absorbs about a quarter of the total, while annually ¥10-20 billion of exports go to each of the following countries: Hongkong, West Germany, Netherlands, Nigeria, Switzerland and Taiwan. Smaller amounts are exported to the Philippines, Canada, Singapore, Australia, and Papua New Guinea. Pearls account for most of West Germany's and Switzerland's imports and about one-third of Hongkong's, while fat and oils account for nearly all of the Netherlands'. Taiwan's imports from Japan consists almost entirely of fishmeal. Exports to the Philippines are virtually all canned mackerel and sardines.

The Japanese fishing industry faces the possibility of a long-term stagnant domestic market due to competition from livestock products whose prices have remained fairly stable, in contrast to fish prices which have risen steadily. Since 1975 the consumer price index for fish (1975 = 100) has risen to 162, while the price of food in general has risen only to 135 and that of meat to only 110.

Currently, fish is the source of about half of the protein in the Japanese diet, down from 80% in 1955. This compares to 65.5% for South Korea, 58.2% for the Philippines, 36.7% for the Soviet Union and 19.8% for Spain. The Japanese fishing industry is now engaging in a publicity campaign to promote fish as a food low in cholesterol, rich in vitamins and low in calories, in order to prevent a further erosion of consumer preference.

The most formidable external competitor to the Japanese fishing industry is South Korea, with which Japan shares offshore waters. Having been forced out of important distant fishing zones, Japanese and South Korean fishing boats have intensified their operations in their joint waters. One of the drawbacks of slimming down the Japanese fishing industry, according to industry sources, is the possibility of South Korea — and to a lesser extent Taiwan — dominating the nearby fishing grounds.

Japanese companies have invested in 97 foreign joint ventures in Asia and the Pacific and 175 worldwide. This represents total investment on the Japanese side amounting to US$101 million as of March 1983, while Japanese investment in Asia and the Pacific alone amounted to US$29 million. Investment by local interests in such joint ventures is about US$150 million. In Asia, South Korea and Indonesia have the most Japanese-participating ventures, 19 and 16 respectively. There are 21 joint trawl-netting ventures in Asia and the Pacific, as well as five ventures seeking tuna and bonito. These represent by far the bulk of Japanese investment.

The proliferation of joint ventures in Asia began in the mid-1970s but reached a peak in 1980 when 113 were in operation. Since then, there has been a steady decline. The number of joint aquaculture ventures has been fairly stable at around 30 for the past seven years. Japanese sources say that trawling joint ventures will continue to decline because of the dull market, especially for shrimps, in Japan; the tendency of Southeast Asian countries to operate fully controlled ventures once their personnel have been trained, and the rising fees for entering foreign waters.

There has also been trouble between Japan and the Soviet Union over Japanese access to Soviet salmon-fishing grounds. Last year some Japanese vessels were caught surreptitiously entering Soviet restricted grounds and had to pay compensation and offer an apology. The Soviets claim that salmon caught by the Japanese in the northwest Pacific belongs to the Soviets because it was spawned in Soviet rivers. The Japanese have requested additional fishing rights. The issue is still pending and Japanese fishing experts regard it as "very delicate."

The constraints on the Japanese fishing industry, along with improved productivity as a result of advanced equipment and techniques, have forced a steady trimming in the number of workers. In 1960, the fishing industry employed about 750,000 people and 90% of fishing enterprises were family units. In a gradual decline, the number of fishery workers currently numbers 460,000, with the majority of the losses coming from small and medium enterprises but not single household units engaged in coastal fishing.

About 200,000 household units are thus engaged, but about a quarter of them are part-timers whose main source of income is elsewhere. Additionally, there are 56,000 fish retail units, 1,266 ice-making plants, 1,795 freezing plants, 22,500 fish-processing plants and 1,111 wholesale markets. All told, the related activities employ 1.38 million people. The elimination of jobs in both the fishing industry and related sectors has not been an important social problem because of Japan's ample labour opportunities, which have led to an unemployment rate stabilising at 2-2.5%.

The efficiency and high technical level of Japan's fishing-industry workers have been improving mainly due the existence of an elaborate educational system. There are 52 fisheries high schools and 17 fisheries colleges. In addition, the responsible ministry attracts some of the best graduates of the science faculties of leading universities. Technical help and consultation are also available from 147 fishery-expertise extension offices throughout the country.

Japan fields more than 410,000 mechanised fishing vessels, of which 7,500 weigh more than 50 gross registered tons. The government offers aid to the fishing industry by providing loans through its banking institutions and by providing capital for building infrastructure such as piers, training centres and research facilities. The total government budget for all fishery-related expenditure in 1983 was about ¥300 billion. The government also establishes broad policy guidelines, the latest of which are to eliminate over-capacity in the industry, deal with the 200-mi fishing limits in an effective way and nurture and replenish fishing grounds.

Six fishing companies are listed on the first section of the Tokyo Stock Exchange. Most have diversified into related areas such as marine transport, chilled and frozen foods and trading, but their profitability is still affected by the vagaries of fish prices. The two biggest conglomerates are Nippon Suisan and Taiyo Fishery, both of which have experienced flat profits or occasional losses since 1980. Nearly all the big companies are reconstructing their divisions to cut costs.

Processing and fishing are usually done by separate enterprises, except in the case of the giant companies which invariably not only do their own processing but also purchase fish from smaller operators. ☐

Scuttling itself by polluting and over-fishing

By Andrew Tanzer in Taipei

From the air, Taiwan's verdant western coast appears to be dotted with thousands of tiny lakes. But the lakes are in fact fishponds. Each year, fish farmers ship millions of eels and shrimp to Japan from fresh- and brackish-water ponds. But Taiwan's technically sophisticated and lucrative aquaculture sector is one of few bright spots in the island's troubled fishing industry.

After decades as an agricultural star performer, the industry has lost its lustre in recent years. A series of blows, including soaring fuel and labour costs, has buffeted it. The island is just coming to grips with expanded territorial waters of nations bordering the Pacific, a problem which has robbed local fishermen of traditional fishing grounds. Closer to home, Taiwan is digging its own grave by polluting and over-fishing coastal waters.

But the US$1.5 billion industry is still an important one. Fish production in 1983 inched up 0.9% to 930,582 tonnes, a shade below the peak year of 1980. During 1973-82, the deep-sea catch actually declined, but aquaculture's output doubled and now accounts for 23% of total production and 35% of production value. The catch from inshore fisheries, mostly nearby waters but defined as using powered vessels of less than 50 tons, has risen modestly.

The industry provides employment for 313,000 people, nearly a quarter of them fish farmers, and contributes 22% of agricultural production value, more than double the share 15 years ago. Exports of fish products in 1982 reached NT$27 billion (US$675 million), up 10-fold in a decade. Per capita consumption of fish in Taiwan is 36 kgs a year and the food provides 10.5 g of protein a day, or one-third of daily consumption of animal protein.

Agricultural planners expect domestic fish consumption to rise slowly to 43 kgs per head by 1992, but that is the least of the industry's problems. Fishing-boat operators' margins have been squeezed by higher (though government-subsided) fuel costs and labour costs which

have been bid up in a tight labour market. Owners have trouble luring manpower away from more secure and less strenuous jobs in the island's booming industrial and service sectors. Boat crews are typically paid a bonus share based on a percentage of catch on top of a monthly salary of about NT$10,000 stipulated by the government. According to one major fleet owner, this year fishermen on deep-sea voyages can expect to net about NT$20,000 a month.

Some boat owners are cutting labour costs by buying more mechanised vessels — for example, tuna companies are substituting purse-seiners for long-liners. But with return on capital low, the industry suffers from an antiquated fleet (mostly locally built) and low investment levels. Capital investment peaked at NT$7.3 billion in 1979 and reached only NT$4.4 billion in 1982. By one account, the island's fleet of tuna boats has dwindled from 700 vessels in the 1970s to 500. The government is encouraging modernisation — but not expansion — of the fleet by providing low-interest loans to owners who retire superannuated boats in favour of new ones. Three government-owned banks extend term loans at about two percentage points below the market rate directly to shipowners or through credit cooperatives in fishermen's associations.

The small size of fishing companies frustrates the introduction of new technology and management. Most owners operate only one vessel, though some deep-sea outfits have as many as 20. The government favours merging but hurts its own case through tax policy: a new company receives a five-year tax exemption on operation of its first vessel, but only four years for succeeding boats. So owners start up new companies for each boat they launch.

Few fishing companies get involved in marketing or fish-processing, leaving this business to food processors. The deep-sea fleet sells the lion's share of its catch to Japanese trading companies and foreign canneries at overseas bases. The industry, wary of market control exerted by the giant Japanese trading houses, is beginning to handle more of

FISHERIES PRODUCTION

Quantity (*thousand tonnes*) Value (*NT$ billion*)	1978		1979		1980		1981		1982		1983	
Unit:	Quantity	Value	Quantity	Value	Quantity	Value	Quantity	Value	Quantity	Value	Quantity	Value
Deep-sea fisheries	335.14	8.76	362.27	10.94	370.34	13.72	338.78	15.60	340.14	17.02	—	—
Inshore fisheries	353.53	9.19	350.80	12.13	358.21	16.09	334.85	16.54	326.51	16.61	—	—
Coastal fisheries*	31.97	1.07	32.57	1.18	32.78	1.21	36.12	1.72	39.44	2.09	—	—
Aquaculture	164.41	12.80	183.69	14.73	175.01	15.07	201.93	16.49	216.44	20.38	—	—
Grand Total	885.04	31.81	929.33	38.97	936.33	46.09	911.68	50.35	922.52	56.10	930.58	—

*Using non-powered boats

Source: Taiwan Fisheries Bureau, Provincial Government.

the marketing. FCF, founded in 1973 by Chang Kuo-an, the president of local Honda motorcar assembler San Yang Industrial Co., already claims a 40% share of Taiwan's tuna exports via its 14 overseas branches.

Most of the inshore catch is sold at home at daily auctions managed by fishermen's associations in production areas. Fish prices are relatively high, reflecting strong demand and protection of the industry. Imports of some inexpensive fish, such as herring and mackerel, are banned as are shipments of pomfret and squid which would compete with the catch of local fishermen. In 1982, more than 90% of Taiwan's imports of 250,000 tonnes of fish products consisted of fishmeal and the industry chalked up a trade surplus of NT$20 billion.

The small size of deep-sea fishing firms bedevils efforts to enter joint ventures with foreign companies — a matter of vital importance since the declaration of 200-mi economic zones by many littoral countries in recent years. At a stroke, the industry lost waters it had fished in for centuries in the Bashi Channel and Sulu and Celebes seas.

Taiwan's lack of diplomatic relations with most countries complicates negotiation of fishing agreements and most talks are handled by fishermen's associations. Taiwan and the Philippines still make overlapping claims to territorial waters in the Bashi Channel. Taiwan and Japan have a tacit agreement to fish in each other's waters. Taiwan fishermen hold sway over the island's coastal waters, but these are beginning to suffer from over-fishing and severe pollution, particularly off the western coast of Taiwan where most of the population and industry is concentrated. Culture of shrimp, oysters and crab in tidal areas has been especially devastated. None of the island's rivers is fit for fish to live in.

The problem of pollution is only now being addressed, but environmental protection — and agricultural interests — almost always take a back seat to industrial development in Taiwan. Luxuries such as clean water have been sacrificed in the name of economic growth (industrial products account for 93% of the island's exports). Agricultural planners complain that existing pollution-control rules are too lax and not rigidly enforced anyway.

If fishermen sacrifice millions of dollars of production a year to industrial interests, they also hurt their own cause by overfishing coastal waters. The government and fishermen's associations have recently begun taking action by defining 21 conservation areas, limiting the size of fish nets, releasing fish fry into the waters and forbidding introduction of new boats of 100-700 tons unless they replace retired vessels.

Set against the gloom in the deep-sea and inshore sectors, aquaculture's rise has been all the more conspicuous. For centuries, milkfish and other species have been considered traditional aquacultural fish, but only in recent years have technological advances transformed fish-farming into a booming export industry. Annual exports of eels to Japan (95% of the crop at NT$400 a kg), where they are considered almost a staple, are running at about US$200 million (3% of total production; 15% of value); shrimp shipments (NT$300 a kg) last year reached US$100 million.

Raising fish in fresh- and brackish-water ponds is expensive — the fish are pampered with large inputs of labour and energy, feed and even medicine. The secret is to

FISHING IN ASIA

cultivate high value-added products with a ready market.

The government has encouraged farmers to convert rice paddies to fishponds as one way of taking a bite out of the island's chronic rice glut. Taiwan enjoys a comparative advantage in aquaculture — at least vis-à-vis Japan — because many species of fish grow faster in its mild climes than farther north. But the key to success has been a vigorous research and development programme in fish-culture technology, in which Taiwan claims to be a world leader.

Research carried out by the provincial government and by private companies has resulted in high — and rising — yields per ha. For example, artificial propagation know-how has enabled farmers to raise the male ratio of tilapia in their ponds to 95%; males grow faster than females. Industry sources said the island's hatcheries can reproduce

Taiwan aquaculture: heading for the open sea?

all species of fish except eels. The aquaculture sector has also introduced nutritious feed pellets blending fishmeal and grains.

But the expansion of fishponds will be constrained by several factors. One is land: the government has shifted its policy to encourage only conversion of poor fields to fishponds. Production gains will be made through higher unit yields rather than increased acreage. The industry is also energy-intensive. Farmers employ electrified water-wheels to aerate the ponds; production of the artificial feed, which requires blending grains, also guzzles energy. Sewage and chemicals which seep into fishponds from the water table lower the survival rate of fish eggs.

With the expansion of fishponds in jeopardy where can the fish industry turn now? Some agricultural planners think the future may be in farming fish in the sea; producing the fry in hatcheries and releasing them into estuaries and coastal areas. ◻

PART 5

Reading Worksheets

In this part of the unit, you will be putting into practice what we have covered so far, following the sequence of thought that you would normally follow when approaching any reading for an assignment.

Each of the following worksheets gives an essay topic for you to work with, and gives the title of the text that you will find useful.

This is what you will do, *before you read the text*.

1 Look at the **text title**, and decide *what you think the text might be about*. Try to use your own words when doing this. (Do this with your partner.)

2 Look at the **text title** and the **essay topic**. Think about what you know already about the subject of the text, and what you need to know to answer the essay topic. Then ask yourself, '*What do I want to find out from this text?*' Discuss your own suggestion with your partner and make a note of both your suggestions.

3 Then ask '*What key words and key terms will I have to look for to get the information that I need to answer section 2?*'

4 Next look again at the **text title**, and ask '*What question(s) should I ask myself to check that I know the main point of the text?*' Discuss this with your partner, and try to come to an agreed conclusion.

5 Both partners should now turn to the text itself and *scan through the text* to find out what the passage is about, and what the answers to question 3 are. Use the same techniques you practised earlier, reading only the first sentence of each paragraph. Treat this as a race. Which of you can find the information first?

Finally: Check what the other partner has written down. Do you agree with each other? If not, look more carefully at the text, and try to establish who is more correct.

When you have completed all five stages, and the final checking, go on to the next worksheet.

The faster you can work through these exercises, the better.

READING FOR INFORMATION, WORKSHEET A

Text Title: 'Japan Saps the World's Rainforests'.
Essay Topic: 'Discuss the impact of logging on world ecology'.

(Text Title)   1 Look at the text title. What might the text be about? (Don't just write 'Japan is sapping the world's rain forests'—be more precise.)

(Text Title and Essay Topic)   2 Look at the text title, then at the essay topic. What do you want to find out from the text? (How much do you know about Japan's use of wood? Do you need some data?)

      3 What key words and key terms will you look for to help you find the answer to point 2? (*not* 'rainforest')

(Text Title)   4 Look at the text title. What question(s) will you ask yourself to check that you have understood the main point of the text?

(Text)   Now scan the passage.
      5 What are the main points the author makes in the text?
      6 Note the time you have taken to scan the passage.

   Check your answers with your partner. If you disagree, look more carefully at the text to decide who is right.

18   New Scientist 2 April 1987

Japan saps the world's rain forests

Bob Johnstone, Tokyo

A NEW international organisation charged with protecting the world's tropical forests approved its first project last week—a survey of surviving forests. The International Tropical Timber Organisation (ITTO), meeting for the first time at its new headquarters in Yokohama, Japan, postponed discussion of plans for a code of conduct for timber companies.

Rain forests are disappearing at the rate of up to 20 million hectares a year, the size of Great Britain. The World Wildlife Fund International predicts that they could vanish within a few decades.

This would be a "catastrophic loss of biological diversity", says Peter Kramer, the fund's director of conservation. At least half of the world's estimated 30 million species live in tropical forests.

Of 14 initiatives approved by the meeting, the most important was the survey of surviving forests—the first for a decade. Environmental groups were disappointed that the council postponed until a meeting in November discussion of a code of conduct. "It is very important that the ITTO gets its act together as soon as possible," said Charles Secrett of Friends of the Earth International. Environmentalists also criticised 15 countries—four consumers and 11 producers—that had failed to pay their subscriptions. The organisation is owed more than $600 000. The US alone owes $50 000.

Logging the removal of complete trees, currently accounts for at least one quarter of the destruction of tropical forests, according to the environmental groups. When the consequences of logging are taken into account, however, the actual damage is far more serious.

Only a minority of trees in any forest are of commercial value. But carelessly felled trees can damage their neighbours, and the heavy vehicles that drag them away cause

further damage and compact the earth, making it difficult for saplings to take root. In addition, the roads that these vehicles require open up the forest to colonising farmers who destroy the trees to make room for fields.

The damage to rain forests is often too serious for natural regeneration to occur.

Chopsticks are the thin end of the wedge as rain forests are exploited

Replanting programmes rarely succeed.

Logging has reduced the rain forest in the Philippines from 16 million hectares in 1960 to 1 million hectares today. Indonesia is down from 65 million hectares to 20 million hectares. Both countries have recently banned the export of logs. Last week, representatives from the Philippines, Indonesia and Malaysia visited Japan's Environmental Agency to seek the Japanese government's cooperation in the protection of tropical forests.

Japan is currently the largest consumer of tropical timber in the world. Most is imported as logs, which are turned into plywood, often for use in the building industry. Conservationists claim that this is a very wasteful use of a precious resource.

As another instance of waste, they point to the billions of pairs of disposable wooden chopsticks that are thrown away every year. Nevertheless, disposable chopsticks account for only around 0·3 per cent of Japan's total timber consumption and tend to be made from wood that would otherwise be wasted.

Until recently, Japanese conservationists showed little concern about the destruction of the tropical forests in neighbouring countries, concerning themselves rather with domestic problems.

But recently, a series of articles in the Asahi newspaper turned the spotlight on logging in the east Malaysian states of Sarawak and Sabah, where the bulk of Japanese tropical timber originates.

The articles also described the plight of the Penan tribe, in the jungles of Borneo, which is fighting the encroachment of Japanese-financed loggers onto its land.

The Japanese government does not accept that Japan is responsible for the destruction of the forests. "Logging is not the cause," says Isao Takahashi, director of forestry products and the chief Japanese representative at the ITTO meeting. He blames colonising farmers and the removal of trees for firewood.

Takahashi thinks that Southeast Asian countries do not take enough care of the forests after the Japanese-owned and Japanese-financed firms have felled the trees. Nevertheless, the Japanese forestry ministry has sent advisors to the producing countries. In addition, at the opening session of the ITTO meeting, Japan pledged $2 million to its projects fund.

● An innovative project designed to protect one of the last remaining blocks of intact tropical rain forest in West Africa has been saved at the last gasp. As predicted by *New Scientist*, the World Wildlife Fund UK has taken over the Korup project in the Cameroon, the largest scheme managed by Bioresources Ltd, a subsidiary of the troubled environmental pressure group, Earthlife. Besides taking over all Bioresource's projects, the WWF will absorb most of its staff too. □

READING FOR INFORMATION, WORKSHEET B

Text Title: 'A Greener Hue for Development Aid'.
Essay Topic: 'Describe some of the more recent attempts to provide aid to developing countries'.

(Text Title)   1 Look at the text title. What might the text be about?

(Text Title and Essay Topic)   2 Look at the text title, then at the essay topic. What do you want to find out from the text?

3 What key words and key terms will you look for to help you find the answers to point 2?

(Text Title)   4 Look at the text title. What question(s) will you ask yourself to check that you have understood the main point of the text?

(Text)   Now scan the passage.

5 What are the main points the author makes in the text?

6 Note the time you have taken to scan the passage.

Check your answers with your partner. If you disagree, look more carefully at the text to decide who is right.

A greener hue for development aid

On April 10th, the finance ministers and central bankers who make up the development committee of the World Bank and the International Monetary Fund will talk about a working paper that advocates giving environmentalists a greater say in the way development aid is given. They have economic reasons for taking it seriously

Satellite images of the earth make grim viewing. Six million hectares, an area almost the size of Ireland, turns to desert every year. Ten million hectares, an area about as big as Kentucky, of tropical forest is cut down each year. Each year, too, soil erosion, often caused by deforestation, diminishes the world's stock of agricultural land by 20m hectares, an area about half the size of Japan.

Environmental pressure groups have long argued that these problems are as pressing as, say, third-world debt. They maintain that international development banks, the World Bank included, have neglected them in pushing ahead with agricultural, power, transport and other programmes. In consequence, these projects have often had an economically-damaging impact on the countries that they are supposed to benefit.

The tide, for the moment, is running with the greens. Mr Barber Conable, the World Bank's president, wants to see the Bank doing more for the environment. The Bank says it has the equivalent of 150 of its 3,000 staff working full-time on environmental work. But it lacks an environmental department; and the links between its small environmental office—which has no economists—and its policy makers are weak.

Though overstaffed, the Bank does not have the experts it needs to vet and monitor for their environmental effects the 250 or more new projects it approves each year. Next month's meeting of the development committee is likely to recommend the appointment of more environmental specialists—a change that could be fitted into a reorganisation that Mr Conable wants to see completed within the next few months. Once the World Bank has given a lead, other multilateral organisations, such as the Asian Development Bank or the Inter-American Development Bank, can be expected to follow.

Forests first
The first, and easiest, thing that the Bank can do is examine more carefully the environmental impact of the projects it sponsors. Many have attracted criticism. Two examples are the "Polonoroeste" development in north-western Brazil, and the resettlement elsewhere in Indonesia of the inhabitants of overcrowded Java. Both resulted in deforestation and damage to the land, and some avoidable human suffering.

Some dam projects have proved equally unpopular. They nearly always involve resettling many people, often on to nearby slopes, where soil erosion is already a problem. The Okavango delta in Botswana is a casualty of agricultural economists not listening to environmentalists. Overgrazing—encouraged by cattle-ranching projects sponsored by the Bank—is turning it into a wasteland.

Worry about such abuses helped persuade the American Congress last October to require the United States Agency for International Development (USAID) to look at the environmental side of all proposed multilateral aid projects and, if necessary, place them on a watch list. The current list contains 28 such projects, though USAID says that sponsoring banks have now dealt with its objections to several of them. If the agency's objections are not met, it must seek to have

While stocks last . . .

the project opposed. In the World Bank's case, this means wielding America's 20% share of the votes on the Bank's executive board.

Calculating the environmental costs of a project is difficult and expensive, but it can be done. The lessons learnt from recent mistakes have made the task a bit easier. It is now known, for example, that planting fast-growing eucalyptus trees to arrest soil erosion does not always work. The trees inhibit undergrowth and can actually result in fewer roots developing and more erosion. By providing still water, dams can promote the spread of malaria and bilharzia. Safeguards against environmental damage often add only small short-term costs, and can bring much larger later benefits.

The Bank's biggest problem is not convincing the rich donor countries but the poor recipient ones. It can do better by:

● Showing, contrary to popular prejudice, that many environment-protecting projects also make economic sense. A Bank review calculates that reforestation brings in a discounted return to total cost of 10-30%; measures to prevent water supplies being diverted by soil erosion have a comparable return of 15-21%.

● Helping to alleviate poverty, the biggest single cause of environmental destruction. Peasants scratching a living from poor soil often cannot afford to let the land lie fallow. Adjustment loans are now being made by the Bank to encourage governments to remove price controls that hold down the prices paid to farmers.

● Distancing itself from econuts who are uninterested in, even hostile to, economic growth if it disrupts nature in any way at all.

● Making people pay for any harm they do. A logging company will often do damage to the environment which it does not have to pay for. Most countries already recognise this, and charge loggers "stumpage"—a tax on each tree they cut down—or ranchers a grazing tax on each cow they introduce. These taxes almost invariably fail to cover the costs of reinstating the land. A more careful analysis of the costs—using some of the thousands of non-governmental organisations which carry out field-work—would help redress the balance. Governments would find it easier to weigh the cost-benefits of smelly or smoky industries if they knew better what the risks were and what it would cost to reduce the chance of damage being done.

The pressure for change is increasing. The UN-backed Brundtland Report on the Environment and Development, due out on April 27th, will give the debate on environmental damage a boost. Commercial banks and lending agencies realise that they cannot afford not to listen.

The fury of Senator Robert Kasten, a Wisconsin Republican, at the damage done by Polonoroeste helped persuade Congress to chop $450m off the Reagan administration's request last October for $1.4 billion for development banks. An ever-greener Congress could soon begin to demand that responsible environmental policies by recipient countries become a condition of loans being made; and that funding for projects in other countries which fail to measure up to America's strict rules on environmental protection should be blocked. If that happens, a number of now-routine industrial projects would be outlawed, as would the use of pesticides like DDT.

READING FOR INFORMATION, WORKSHEET C

Text Title: 'Nailing the Mercury'.
Essay Topic: 'Drug abuse in the developed world'.

(Text Title)   1 Look at the text title. What might the text be about?

(Text Title   2 Look at the text title, then at the essay topic. What do you want to find out from
and   the text?
Essay Topic)
                   3 What key words and key terms will you look for to help you find the answers to
                     point 2?

(Text Title)   4 Look at the text title. What question(s) will you ask yourself to check that you
                     have understood the main point of the text?

(Text)   Now scan the passage.

                   5 What are the main points the author makes in the text?

                   6 Note the time you have taken to scan the passage.

   Check your answers with your partner. If you disagree, look more carefully at the text to
decide who is right.

Nailing the mercury

**British drug abuse is on the increase. The government's fight against it
would be helped if it paid less attention to cannabis, and more to alcohol**

How many Britons are addicted to hard drugs? Nobody knows for sure. The Home Office figure for new and existing notified narcotic addicts in 1985 is around 15,000—three times as many as in 1979. Most researchers reckon the Home Office figures understate the total by between five and ten times, so the true number may be over 100,000. More accurate figures could be found only through a national survey—which Britain, unlike most other countries, has never had.

Heroin has been responsible for most of the 1980s' rise in hard-drug abuse. But evidence from drug seizures (see chart) suggests its use may be levelling off. Meanwhile, police and customs officers grimly await the much-heralded upsurge in cocaine abuse as the powerful Latin American producers switch from the saturated American market to Europe. Cocaine's street price in London has fallen to around £50 a gram, though that is still high relative to other drugs. Last December saw the first police seizures of "crack"—a highly addictive compound of cocaine and baking soda which has been spreading frighteningly fast across America. And addiction to amphetamines ("speed"), which are increasingly injected rather than swallowed or sniffed, is also growing fast .

So far, the government has concentrated mainly on stamping out the supply of illegal drugs, rather than trying to reduce the demand for them. Mr David Mellor, the Home Office minister who chairs the ministerial group on drug misuse, is now cautiously optimistic about the fight against the traffickers. Big producer countries like Pakistan and India have become more helpful since they themselves started to suffer from drug abuse. The 1986 Drug Trafficking Offences Act made it possible for the police to confiscate the proceeds of drug dealers. And international police and customs co-operation is improving.

Economics being what it is, though, demand for hard drugs will always call forth supply. Recent falls in street prices of most hard drugs show how difficult it is to block supplies—one drug expert has likened it to nailing a blob of mercury to the floor. So what about trying to cut demand? The government's £2m publicity campaign to discourage heroin abuse has had a mixed reception. Health-edu-cation professionals always feared it might interest rather than deter potential abusers, which is one reason why the health department ran it itself rather than entrust it to the now-defunct Health Education Council. It is too early to be sure, but the evidence so far seems to justify the professionals' scepticism.

Experts argue about the best treatment for addicts. In the 1960s, addicts usually went to specialised drug clinics. Now, more than half go to their family doctors, or general practitioners. GPs are often inadequately trained in both the handling and the treatment of this awkward group of patients. Most doctors are no longer allowed to prescribe heroin, so they put their patients on methadone instead. Methadone gives less of a buzz than heroin, so some addicts drift back to the streets to get their fixes. For those who do not, methadone addiction itself is increasingly a problem: for example, Washington DC now has more methadone than heroin addicts. Some experts therefore advocate a return to freer heroin-prescribing.

Other men's poisons

The biggest anomaly in the government's drugs policy remains its treatment of cannabis and alcohol. Britain has the stiffest laws on personal consumption of cannabis in Western Europe. Police and customs officers rigidly enforce them—sometimes at the cost of creating problems with black communities. Court proceedings on drugs are dominated by cannabis: 88% of drug convictions in

Alcohol kills more people

1985 were for cannabis possession, compared with 43% in 1967.

Yet medical opinion on cannabis is almost unanimous: it is less addictive than alcohol and does less harm to health than tobacco. Hence the steady campaign to legalise the stuff—or at least decriminalise it (ie, make possession, as opposed to dealing, no longer a criminal offence). Fears that legalising cannabis would lead to an explosion of pot-smoking seem exaggerated. In Holland, controlled legalisation of cannabis in 1982 has actually reduced its use. A 1983 survey recorded only 2% of 13- to 25-year-olds using cannabis, compared with 15% in 1976.

The British government's seeming indifference to alcohol abuse is even more extraordinary. Alcohol causes 100 times more premature deaths than hard drugs. Consumption has increased steadily since the 1950s, particularly among the young. Alcohol may act as a "gateway" to other drugs, including heroin. And whereas heroin and cocaine abusers damage only themselves, heavy drinkers damage others—in car accidents or football hooliganism, for example. Yet the government has no anti-alcohol campaign to match its anti-smoking and anti-drugs ones. In his last budget, the chancellor of the exchequer, Mr Nigel Lawson, refused to put up excise taxes on drink, which means that the real rate of taxes on them has gone down. Society's amused tolerance of alcohol abuse makes it harder to persuade other drug abusers of their dangerous folly.

UK drug seizures by weight

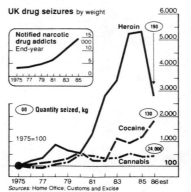

Notified narcotic drug addicts
End-year

Heroin 190

Quantity seized, kg

Cocaine 130

Cannabis 100

1975=100

24,000

1975 77 79 81 83 85 86 est
Sources: Home Office; Customs and Excise

THE ECONOMIST APRIL 18 1987

READING FOR INFORMATION, WORKSHEET D

Text Title: 'African Immunization Year, 1986'.
Essay Topic: 'Describe attempts currently being made to combat disease in African countries'.

(Text Title)	1 Look at the text title. What might the text be about?
(Text Title and Essay Topic)	2 Look at the text title, then at the essay topic. What do you want to find out from the text?
	3 What key words and key terms will you look for to help you find the answers to point 2?
(Text Title)	4 Look at the text title. What question(s) will you ask yourself to check that you have understood the main point of the text?
(Text)	Now scan the passage.
	5 What are the main points the author makes in the text?
	6 Note the time you have taken to scan the passage.

Check your answers with your partner. If you disagree, look more carefully at the text to decide who is right.

Expanded Programme on Immunization

African Immunization Year, 1986

By declaring 1986 as African Immunization Year, the African Regional Committee has challenged member countries to ensure the protection of their children against six killer diseases

by Dr L. A. Arevshatian

Regional Officer for the Expanded Programme on Immunization, WHO Regional Office for Africa

The African Region is the true homeland of WHO's Expanded Programme on Immunization (EPI), which held its very first seminar in Kumasi, Ghana, in 1974. It is not perhaps something of which we should be proud, since it was born out of suffering. Yet we are proud, and rightly so, because EPI is directed towards reducing that suffering. However, the struggle in Africa is a hard and complex one because of widespread malnutrition, poor resources and enormous logistical problems.

Without immunization, one million African children south of the Sahara will die before their first birthday from diseases that could have been prevented. A further half-million will be disabled each year. And this is not all: hundreds of thousands of African mothers and fathers will spend several days taking care of 32 million episodes of sickness in their babies every year, due to measles, tuberculosis, pertussis, tetanus, diphtheria and poliomyelitis—all of which diseases are covered by EPI.

The severity and huge toll of these diseases in Africa is the result of a vicious cycle of infection and malnutrition. Immunization services are effective in preventing specific diseases which might otherwise precipitate malnutrition. They therefore contribute significantly to reducing childhood mortality and disability. For example, the pre-

sent immunization coverage of 20 per cent of the target population of children aged under one year will prevent six million cases in the Region, thereby saving 200,000 lives and 100,000 cases of disability.

That in itself is already a significant achievement. Yet it is as nothing compared to the 32 million cases expected

A Kenyan baby receives its protecting dose of oral vaccine against polio.

Photo WHO/Jorgen Schytte

to occur each year. Even with the present coverage, 2,200 African children still die every day because they are not protected by immunization.

It is against this background that the African Regional Committee, at its thirty-fifth meeting in Lusaka, Zambia, last September, adopted a special

resolution proclaiming 1986 as African Immunization Year. It invited member states to step up their EPI activities with a view to achieving the programme's objective by 1990. This calls for the provision of immunization to all children and all women of child-bearing age.

There are many constraints in the way of achieving that objective. Tropical temperatures can diminish the potency of vaccines even in the space of a single vaccination session; there may be a lack of electric power, inadequate transportation facilities and equipment, manpower shortage and so on. These all pose special challenges for many national programmes, especially in West Africa where the per capita income is much lower than elsewhere in the continent.

At a time when health services in Africa are striving to administer three, or at the minimum two, injections to children, their counterparts in the developed world have little difficulty in giving 10 or 12 such injections to protect children throughout their lives not only against all six EPI target diseases but also against mumps and rubella.

Since the inauguration of EPI in the Region in 1977, progress has been made in establishing immunization as an essential component of primary health care (PHC). The programme was received throughout the Region with remarkable enthusiasm and determination. In 1983, the latest year for which comprehensive country data are available, 31 per cent of children aged under one year received the first dose of diphtheria/pertussis/tetanus vaccine (DPT-1), which is an indicator of access to immunization services, while 20 per cent received DPT-3, an indicator of full immunization. The tragedy is that vaccination, one of most powerful and effective tools in preventive medicine, is not yet available to most children in Africa.

The objective of African Immunization Year is to substantially increase immunization coverage among the target population and build up a mechanism for permanent services. While the proposed objectives are common to the countries of the Region, the targets actually set and the strategies adopted differ according to existing EPI coverage and the degree of integration of the programme into PHC. Some of the most successful strategies and approaches being employed in this crucial year have laid emphasis on intersectoral collaboration, setting-up of national EPI committees, winning over political and religious leaders, providing immuniz-ation at all health contact points, giving priority to large urban areas, concentrat-ing scarce resources on the new-born to 11-month-old age group (the most vulnerable of all), and increasing out-reach vaccination sessions for the most peripheral populations. Arranging per-iodic immunization rounds and national immunization days has proved very ac-ceptable to the populations as well as to the health services.

Many favourable factors can contri-bute to the success of EPI in the Region as a whole, and of African Immunization Year in particular. For instance, Africa was the last active participant in the smallpox eradication programme, which resulted in the health services accumulating valuable experience and created a pool of skilled national experts in and managers of disease control. There is a strenuous political commit-ment in several countries, where Heads of State and other high-level officials are giving their personal support to immunization. As a result of the procla-mation of African Immunization Year, this commitment is increasing in other countries of the Region.

Immunization in Africa is not a pro-gramme for individuals; rather it is a family and community one. Experience in several countries shows that, if prop-erly managed, the community can par-ticipate actively at all stages of pro-gramme activities, including planning and evaluation. African Immunization Year has won maximum recognition from the international community, alongside UNICEF's outstanding support to the universal child immunization ap-proach. International and bilateral agen-cies and non-governmental organiz-ations (NGOs), such as UNDP, Save the Children Fund, Rotary International and some international development agen-cies, have contributed funds, technical staff, vaccines and cold chain equip-ment.

WHO and UNICEF are committed to achieving the goal of making immuniz-ation available to all children by 1990. Their collaboration is complementary. While UNICEF is increasing its financial, material and manpower support to na-tional immunization programmes, WHO in the African Region is introducing new and more flexible organizational struc-tures which will permit closer contacts with the countries at subregional and country levels. This will considerably increase the flow of technical expertise from WHO to each country, thereby improving the managerial capabilities of

Immunizations are part of primary health care activities and require a strong involve-ment of the community.   Photo WHO H. Anenden

national programme personnel at all levels.

We intend to focus on the district level as the main operational support to immunization programmes. This sup-port will not be limited to the delivery of immunization alone but will include oral rehydration for diarrhoeal diseases, malaria treatment and prophylaxis, ad-vising on breastfeeding and weaning, clean water and sanitation and other elements of primary health care. So African Immunization Year will become one of the innovative mechanisms which strengthens the existing health infrastructure and promotes the primary health care approach to Health for all by the year 2000.

The concept of African Immunization Year calls for careful thought and plan-ning. It is viewed in the context of the regional medium-term programme, so planning for a single year is not enough. Plans have been drawn up in many countries to cover at least four or five years, with 1986 as the key year of the overall plan.

The most successful programmes are those for which all national and external resources human, financial and material can be listed sector by sector or agency by agency. Accord-ingly, all the participants in the pro-gramme are aware of their responsibil-ities, and of the precise amount and type of support expected of them. Posters, booklets, slide sets, films and other health education materials have been prepared to inform the population about immunization and motivate them.

A number of countries have issued such materials in local languages, thereby considerably increasing com-munity involvement.

District level operation support teams have been created which will carry out immunizations in conjunction with other PHC activities, and not as a "vertical" and isolated activity. EPI has often proved to be an effective entry point for other primary health care activities, especially those related to child survival as defined in the Declaration of Alma-Ata.

Training is regarded as crucial for African Immunization Year. Many Afri-can countries are running training courses and seminars for middle-level management and peripheral-level per-sonnel. WHO Headquarters in Geneva and the African Regional Office in Braz-zaville provide course materials and staff to strengthen the technological aspects of national training pro-grammes.

Working with national auth-orities, UNICEF is making tremendous efforts to provide not only vaccines but also cold chain and immunization equip-ment. WHO and other agencies also collaborate with nationals in supplying vaccines and equipment, as well as technical advice on the selection of vaccines and materials. National EPI programme managers' meetings are being arranged in English-speaking and French-speaking Africa.

African Immunization Year, will put the spotlight on the Expanded Pro-gramme on Immunization. But that pro-gramme will not end in December nor even next year. It will continue as long as children are being born, so the activities of EPI must be considered as being of a permanent nature.   ∎

Below is a blank reading worksheet. Prepare one for yourself and use it with one of your readings in your major subjects.

Use it like this: where it says *Text Title*, write the title of the chapter or the article you are about to read. Where it says *Essay Topic*, write the title of the assignment you have been set. Then go through the various stages set out in the worksheet.

READING FOR INFORMATION, WORKSHEET E

Text Title:
Essay Topic:

(*Text Title*)	1 Look at the text title. What might the text be about?
(*Text Title and Essay Topic*)	2 Look at the text title, then at the essay topic. What do you want to find out from the text?
	3 What key words and key terms will you look for to help you find the answers to point 2?
(*Text Title*)	4 Look at the text title. What question(s) will you ask yourself to check that you have understood the main point of the text?
(*Text*)	Now scan the passage.
	5 What are the main points the author makes in the text?

UNIT 5

Notetaking Skills

Do your lecture notes look like this? If they do, this unit is for *you*!

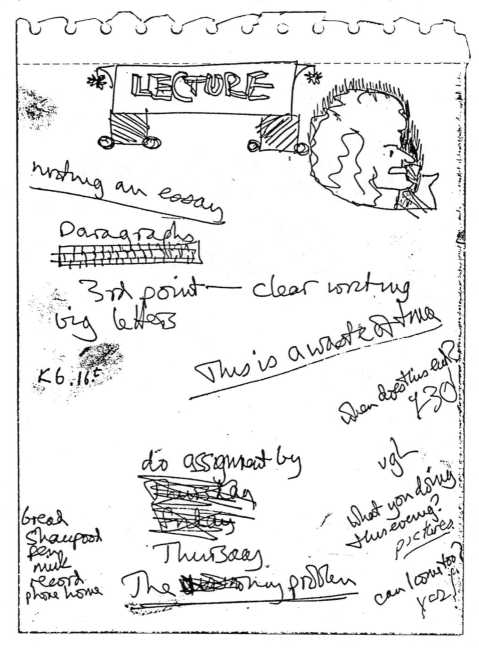

You will take a large number of notes in your time as a student. However, unless you have a good technique most, if not all, of the notes you take will be a waste of time. There are several golden rules about notetaking that you should have firmly fixed in your mind before you begin to take any notes at all.

PART 1

Six Ways to Successful Notetaking

Here are some 'golden rules' to help you take successful notes.

GOLDEN RULE—1

Clarify your purpose.

Before you begin, ask yourself why you are taking the notes.

Do you really need to write notes on everything in front of you?

You have selected an article from a journal, and you are all set to make notes for an essay. Should you take notes on the whole article, or only on part of it?

Write down all the occasions you can think of when you need to write notes on the *whole* of a chapter or the *whole* of a book or lecture.

Discuss these with a partner. Do you agree with what your partner has written?

Hopefully this will show you that there are very few times when you have to make notes on a whole text. Usually you are looking for *specific information* when you read, and the kind of notes you take should reflect this.

List below as many situations as you can think of, where you need to take notes.

What kind of notes would you take? Would you take different kinds of notes for different occasions?

Example:

Situation	*Type of notes*
shopping	list of single words

GOLDEN RULE—2

Write all your notes on the same sized paper.

You will take better notes, and you are more likely to use them at a later date (when revising for exams, for instance) if they look neat. One of the first rules for neatness is to write everything on sheets of paper all of the same size. It doesn't matter what size you choose, but once you have decided, stick to it! *Never* write notes on odd scraps of paper.

Once you have decided on paper size, then try to store them in a proper file.

What size paper do you prefer? Write down the paper size you will be using in future. (If you're not sure of the paper size, your tutor will help you.)

GOLDEN RULE—3

When you begin, lay out your notes properly. Make a full record of the source of the notes you are writing, at the top of the first page.

If you are listening to a lecture, write
- the name of the course;
- the date of the lecture;
- the title of the lecture;
- the name of the lecturer.

If you are reading a book or a periodical article, write
- the name of the author;
- the date of publication;
- the title of the book (or journal);
- the name of the publisher (or, in the case of an article, the volume number);
- the page number(s).

How to find these details is discussed briefly in Unit 3: Library Skills. This will be discussed at greater length in the Unit 7: Quoting Skills.

If the book or journal is a library book, **write down the library catalogue number**. Below there are some examples of how to do this.

If you write down all this information *before* you begin making notes, you will save yourself a great deal of time later on. This is for two reasons: first, you will be expected to name the source of your information in the bibliography at the end of your essay; and, second, if the book or article is a useful one, you may want to look at it again. Unless you have already noted down the information, both of these reasons involve you going back to look for the book again! Why waste half of an hour of your time going to the library because you have to trace the book through the library catalogue, when you could have all the information at your fingertips?

Here are some examples of how to lay out the beginning of your notes.

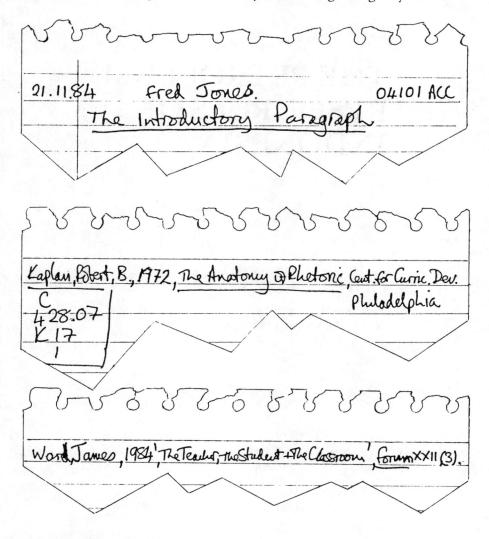

21.11.84   Fred Jones.   04101 ACC
The Introductory Paragraph

Kaplan, Robert, B., 1972, The Anatomy of Rhetoric, Cent. for Curric. Dev.
                                                    Philadelphia
C
428.07
K 17
1

Ward, James, 1984 'The Teacher, the Student + the Classroom', Forum XXII (3).

EXERCISE 5.1

1 Write a notes heading for this lesson.
2 Do one for the lesson before this one.
3 Think about your course so far. How will you label: (a) the courses; and (b) the individual teaching sessions? With a partner, try to go through all the lessons you have had over the last week and decide the best label for each one.
4 Look at the following books. How will you write a notes heading for each of them? The arrow indicates the chapter you are about to read in the case of the book, and the article in the case of the journal.

THE PETROLEUM RESOURCES OF INDONESIA

OOI JIN BEE

Professor of Geography
National University of Singapore

Issued under the auspices of the
Institute of Southeast Asian Studies in Singapore

KUALA LUMPUR
OXFORD UNIVERSITY PRESS
OXFORD NEW YORK MELBOURNE
1982

Oxford University Press
Oxford London Glasgow
New York Toronto Melbourne Auckland
Kuala Lumpur Singapore Hong Kong Tokyo
Delhi Bombay Calcutta Madras Karachi
Nairobi Dar es Salaam Cape Town

and associates in

Beirut Berlin Ibadan Mexico City Nicosia

● *Oxford University Press 1982*

ISBN 0 19 582527 6

Printed in Singapore by Koon Wah Printing (Pte) Ltd.
Published by Oxford University Press, 3, Jalan 13/3,
Petaling Jaya, Selangor, Malaysia.

Contents

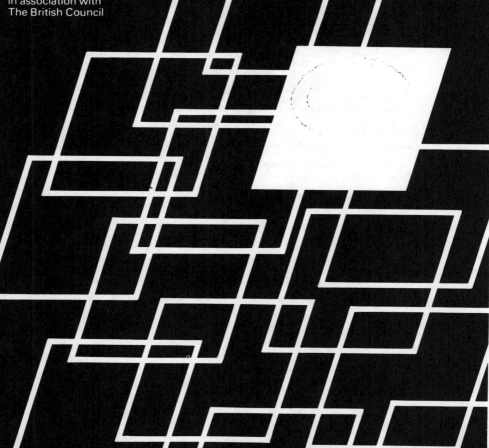

ELT
JOURNAL

VOLUME 39/1
JANUARY 1985

An international journal for
teachers of English to speakers
of other languages

Oxford University Press
in association with
The British Council

Contents

ELT Journal   *Volume 39   Number 1   January 1985*

GOLDEN RULE—4

Use the title of the chapter or lecture to help you anticipate the main ideas of the text.

In Unit 4: Reading Skills you practised looking at chapter titles to anticipate what the chapter might be about, and later to check if you had understood the main points of the chapter.

If you are looking for specific information, then it is important that you examine the titles of possible sources so that you do not waste time making notes on irrelevant things.

If you are still not clear about how to do this, look again at the relevant section of Reading Skills *before* you do the next exercise.

EXERCISE 5.2

Look at the chapter titles and lecture titles below, and try to decide what questions you can ask yourself about the titles to help you spot the main point of the text.

1 Urban Bias and Food Policy in Poor Countries
2 Increasing the Harvest
3 A Fresh Look at Early Man
4 Food First
5 A Tale of Three Villages
6 Problems of the Aid Recipient Country
7 Forms of Aid: Population Control
8 Prehistoric Man in the New World
9 A Mystery and a Theory
10 Current Arguments on Early Man

GOLDEN RULE—5

Keep your own ideas separate from those in the text.

You may need to read your notes again, either for a later piece of work or for revision. In either case, it may be a year or more between the time you write the notes and the time you reread them. You cannot hope to remember what was in the text and what were your own comments on it.

REMEMBER: Your task is to write what is in the text, whether you agree with it or not.

If you want to comment on what you are reading or hearing—to tell yourself to refer to another book, perhaps, or to disagree with what you are writing down—then write your comments down, and draw a box around them:

RELC, 1979, Guidelines for Communication Activities, SEAMEO, Singapore.

Ch. 1. Communic. Competence + Lang Teaching   p. 1 - 21.
    by Christina Bratt Paulston.

Intro
    increasing concern for communic. comp. of sts.

C.C = can be 2 things!

    Rivers (73) + EFL's in US = 'linguistic interaction in target lang'

        ESL = Hymes (1972) = lang + social rules etc.
                1.e. socio - cultural rules for language
                    as import. as lang.
                    ┌─────────────────────────────────────┐
                    │ But is there time to cover both?   │
                    └─────────────────────────────────────┘

        grammar texts = Rivers et al
    notional/functional syllabus = Hymes et al
                    ┌──────────────────────────────┐
                    │ check notional/functional!   │
                    └──────────────────────────────┘

    e.g. of social rules for lang. use.
            wh questions   but what about quis you
                                    can't ask.
                                    eg (for English people) 'what do you earn
                                    a year?' = polite in Asia
                                    eg age questions in Japan OK.
                                        not UK.
                        ┌─────────────────────────────────────┐
                        │ isn't this too culturally bound?   │
                        │ what about ESL students — they   │
                        │ don't need to know about British   │
                        │ social rules.   │
                        └─────────────────────────────────────┘

EXERCISE 5.3

Look at the last set of notes you wrote for one of your specialist subjects. Did you write any of your own comments in your notes? If so, go through the notes and put a box around each of your comments while you can still remember what were *your own ideas* and what were ideas from the text.

GOLDEN RULE—6

When you finish, sum up what you have written.

What do you usually do at the end of a study session? Do you just close your books and walk away? *Don't!* You need something that will round off the session for you and to make sure the material that you have been studying will stay in your memory, at least until you need it again.

There is one very simple thing you should do whenever you finish taking notes on a chapter, or an article in a journal, or when you come to the end of your time at your desk—that is, **sum it up**. No matter how long the text, or how complicated the subject, try to write a summary of the text you have just read, in a few lines, or *at most* one page.

Why is this so important?

(a) It makes you bring together all the ideas you have just been reading about. It will show up what you do not understand, and you can sort it out there and then while everything is fresh in your mind. If you cannot do a summary of what you have just read, you can be sure you haven't really understood it!

(b) When you come to put all your ideas together for that important class paper, or when you come to sit down to revise all your work for the examination, the material is all to hand, neatly summed up on one side of paper, easily digestible. If there is anything you cannot remember when you read your one-page summary, you can quickly go to your notes, or even to the text itself, and sort it out.

Look at the notes you took for the last lecture you attended. Write a summary of the lecture on *one side* of a sheet of paper.

A brief coherent summary is a very useful indicator of how much you have *really* understood.

EXERCISE 5.4

You have been presented with six golden rules. What are they? Write them down.

PART 2

Looking at the Text Itself

Golden Rule–4 suggested that you look at the title of a book or a chapter in a book to find out if it will be suitable for your purpose. Having done this, the next stage is: **look quickly through the text itself to find the relevant section**. After all, you are far too busy to read the whole thing word by word until you find what you are looking for.

Several textual clues are there to help you. The first is in the *print* itself.

Often important points are highlighted in a text by the use of CAPITAL LETTERS or **bold print**. These devices are designed to make certain words stand out from the page, usually because they are important. You can look through a large number of pages very quickly indeed if you are just scanning for words in capitals or in bold print.

REMEMBER: CAPITALS or **bold type** will be your key terms in this particular scanning exercise.

If the text you are reading has either of these devices, then it will make your task of looking for main points very much easier, for the writer will have already isolated the main points of the text for you. Look quickly through the rest of this *Study Skills Handbook*, and see how clearly words in capitals or bold print stand out from the page. In this book, important points are **always** printed in bold type! Other emphasis is given by the use of *italic* print.

Sometimes, however, you will have to read a lengthy text that has no easy textual clues to help you. Instead you will have to rely on your own scanning techniques to help you. This is where your work on key words and key terms will be most useful. Look back at the relevant section in Unit 4: Reading Skills if you are still not quite sure of how to decide on the necessary key words and key terms for a reading passage.

Tackling the Paragraph

All of that which has been discussed so far is very easy if the text is reasonably short and you can look quickly through the whole passage. Sometimes, however, you will have to work through a lengthy text, looking for one short section where the writer is making a particular point.

The most useful way you can deal with lengthy texts is to look closely at the places where **new paragraphs** begin.

LOOK CAREFULLY AT THE FIRST SENTENCE OF EVERY PARAGRAPH.

In the first sentence of every paragraph there is a *paragraph introducer*.

Paragraph introducers will help you scan quickly through a long text. By concentrating initially on the paragraph introducers, you will be able to work out how the text is constructed, and, having done that, you will be able to find those places in the text where the points you are looking for may be found. Once you have identified these places, you will be able to ignore the rest and concentrate only on the few paragraphs that are likely to contain the information you need.

The paragraph introducer is a sentence at the very beginning of a paragraph containing a word or group of words that link the paragraph with the previous ones. Often this first sentence describes what the paragraph is all about.

A word of warning: Although the first sentence of a paragraph will often state the main point of the paragraph, it does not **always** do so! So treat this second feature of the paragraph introducer with care.

Below is a short text showing how the paragraph introducer works.

THE AIMS OF EDUCATION

The aims of education may perhaps be best expressed in three parts as they refer to the individual, to culture and to society.

First, education should be designed so as to provide for each individual the kinds of experiences through which he can achieve the measure of control over this environment of which he is capable. Furthermore, he should be able to determine for himself his own objectives in life and express himself as adequately as his own resources and those of his community will allow.

Secondly, education should produce people who will see that the living cultural tradition of the community is conserved. They should also see to it that opportunity is provided for its enrichment and refinement.

Thirdly, education should aim to ensure that the members of society sufficiently understand the moral and material bases of their societal life. They should be so committed to its welfare that they are able in willing co-operation to command the means and determine the ends whereby it may continually be reconstructed to their mutual benefit.

In this very simple example, the linking phrases in the paragraph introducer should be very clear. They are:

First   Secondly   Thirdly

Of course, there is no paragraph linker in the first paragraph, as there are no earlier paragraphs to link it to.

These linkers help us see that the writer is making *three* points in his short text. If you make notes on this text and only manage to write down two points, you will not have been paying attention to one of the main clues as to what the text is all about.

This was a very simple example, but it demonstrates one type of linking phrase that connects the ideas in one paragraph with the ones that have come before: that of **sequence**. Here are some other linking phrases that often occur.

Sequence	Then . . . Next . . . Finally . . .
Result	Consequently . . . Thus . . . Hence . . .
Contrast	Nevertheless . . . However . . .
	In spite of . . . Although . . .
Addition	Furthermore . . . Moreover . . .
Giving examples	An example . . . One instance . . .
Summing up	Everything so far . . . All of this . . . So . . .

There are, of course, many more types of paragraph linker. The important thing is to be aware that they exist, and that they can be very useful indeed.

Let us look at a longer and slightly more complicated example to see how paragraph linkers are used in practice. Look at the text called 'Breeding Sugar Cane for Energy'.

Scan through the text, looking carefully at the first one or two lines of each paragraph.

EXERCISE 5.5

What are the paragraph linkers of each of the paragraphs in this text? Remember, you must ignore the very first paragraph of any text when you are using paragraph linkers to guide you through a text, as the linkers only refer to the preceding paragraphs. You can only look for linkers from the second paragraph onwards.

Write down the introductory sentence in full, and then below that the linking words or phrases occurring in each of the paragraph introducers. Where you can find none, then write 'none'. As you will see, the **absence** of a linker is just as important as the presence of one.

The first part of the text has been done for you. Try to do the rest.

Paragraph 2

Sentence: Two conditions need to be fulfilled to make it worthwhile to cultivate an agricultural crop for energy.

Linker: None.

Paragraph 3

Sentence: Professor Mike Giamalva and his colleagues at Louisiana State University have now produced a plant that is super-productive.

Linker:

Paragraph 4

Sentence: Another advantage of Giamalva's strain of sugar cane is its high fibre content.

Linker: Another.

Now try to do the same for the rest of the paragraphs.

Did you get them right? Once you have completed this exercise, check against the answers below.

Breeding sugar cane for energy

Peter de Groot

A NEW VARIETY of sugar cane, bred from crosses of ordinary cultivated strains with a wild type found in Argentina, could become an important source of energy as well as sugar (*Biomass*, vol 6, p 61).

Two conditions need to be fulfilled to make it worthwhile to cultivate an agricultural crop for energy. The crop must be easy to harvest and process, and it must be high-yielding. On both these counts, sugar cane is ideal: the technology for harvesting and milling has been thoroughly tested over the years, and sugar cane is one of the most productive plants ever recorded.

Professor Mike Giamalva and his colleagues at Louisiana State University have now produced a plant that is super-productive. Their new variety grows to

Sugar cane: a source of energy

3·6 metres high. On experimental plots, it gives yields of 253 tonnes per hectare—equal to the highest yield of any plant recorded. But even this record has been exceeded. On good soil, yields may reach 321 tonnes per hectare.

Another advantage of Giamalva's new strain of sugar cane is its high fibre content. Traditionally, researchers have selected strains that produce large amounts of juice rich in sugar, and low quantities of fibre. The fibre is either discarded, or sometimes burnt as fuel. The new sugar cane gives exceptional quantities of fibre for only modest amounts of juice. When it comes from the mill, the fibrous residue, known as bagasse, has about 70 per cent of the heat content of wood, or 30-40 per cent of that of coal.

Burning bagasse to provide energy is not a new idea. Many sugar factories throughout the world are now self-sufficient in energy, while some, for example, in Mauritius, Hawaii and South Africa, "export" electricity to the national grid. Mauritius currently gets around 10 per cent of its electricity from sugar factories.

However, in Louisiana local farmers are unwilling to grow the cane until they have a guaranteed market. Yet industrialists will not invest in the new fuel until they have a constant supply. And only local factories may be able to exploit cane because, being bulky, it is costly to transport. One way of overcoming this problem would be to dry the fibrous residue and compact it into pellets or larger briquettes. Work on compacting bagasse is now under way in several research centres. Whether compacting will pay its way will depend on the local situation and the cost of alternative energy supplies. A study carried out by Fay Baguant from the University of Mauritius showed that electricity could be produced there from bagasse pellets about twice as cheaply as from oil or coal-fired stations.

In the future, cane will be more valuable in the production of a liquid fuel. Cane fibres are made up for the most part from lignin and ligno-cellulose (lignin is a natural polymer that gives support and protection to plants and trees). Lignin is broken down naturally by lignase, an enzyme produced by the fungus *Phanerochaete Chrysoporium*. Biochemists are now working on ways of harnessing lignase to break down lignin on a commercial scale (*New Scientist*, 16 May, p 16). When this is achieved, it will be possible to degrade the bulky fibres to produce alcohol and other valuable chemicals.

Giamalva is confident that once the technology for converting the ligno-cellulose in the fibres directly into alcohol has been developed, cane will come into its own.

The new variety can be grown with ordinary sugar cane or with other crops to provide energy for processing. It can be compressed into briquettes and burned as a substitute for charcoal. Or it can be incorporated into paper, cardboard and fibreboard. Brazil, with its fleet of cars running almost entirely on alcohol fuel extracted from sugar cane, already has shown that the plant has the potential to alter radically a country's agricultural sector.   □

ANSWERS

Paragraph 4   The linker is 'Another'.
Paragraph 5   None.
Paragraph 6   The linker is 'However'.
Paragraph 7   The linker is 'In the future'.
Paragraph 8   None.
Paragraph 9   The linker is 'The new variety'.

How do these work?
Look at the linkers again.

Paragraph 2

There are no linkers here. If there are no linkers, it is safe to assume that there are no **direct** links with the paragraph preceding it. Indeed that is true for this text. The introduction explains the background. Paragraph 2 deals with the 'two conditions' which 'need to be fulfilled to make it worthwhile'.

Paragraph 3

There are no linkers here, either. This paragraph does not continue with a discussion with the two conditions but, instead, talks about the **people** who have developed this new strain of sugar cane (and goes on to talk about the cane itself).

Paragraph 4

This paragraph has a linker: 'Another'. The word appears right at the beginning of the paragraph, and this is no accident. It tells the reader that the paragraph to come is **continuing** the discussion covered in the previous paragraph. In this case it continues talking about the advantages of the newly developed crop.
   The writer is telling his readers that these two paragraphs should be seen as two parts of one idea: the advantages of this new crop.

Paragraph 5

There is no linking word here. No link is needed, for a new stage in the narrative begins at this point. The writer is explaining what is *not* new about the new crop.

Paragraph 6

The linking word here is 'However'. A writer begins a paragraph with words like 'however' when he wants to signal to the reader that he is about to begin discussion of problems or disadvantages. This is just what is happening here. The paragraph describes some of the economic problems involved in growing the cane.

Paragraph 7

The linker here is 'In the future'. This indicates another shift in the narrative: the writer is going to talk about future developments.

Paragraph 8

The linker here is a **linguistic** one, hidden in the text: it is 'the' in the phrase 'the ligno-cellulose'. Although a linker of this type is sometimes hard to spot, it is just as important as the more obvious ones. If there were no links between paragraph 8 and paragraph 7, then the sentence would read: '. . . once the technology for converting ligno-cellulose in the fibres . . .

Can you recognize the difference in meaning between the two versions?

The use of 'the' here tells the reader that the topic covered in paragraph 7 is still being discussed.

Paragraph 9

This is the last paragraph: the conclusion. There is a linker here: 'The' in 'The new variety'.

You have to be a little careful with concluding paragraphs, for the link may well be with the whole reading passage rather than the paragraph immediately before: and that is the case here. 'The' refers back to the **whole discussion** about the new crop.

If you look at the whole passage in the light of the way linkers are used, you will see that the passage is constructed like this:

1 **Introduction** (a new sugar cane as a source of energy).
2 **Background** (two conditions needed to make a crop a useful source of energy).

3 **First condition fulfilled** (high yield).
4 **Second condition fulfilled** (ease of processing).

5 **Acceptability of the scheme** (not a new idea to use corn as an energy source).
6 **Problem** (economic factors).

7 **Future development** (of cane as an energy source).
8 **Future development** (continued).

9 **Conclusion** (possible uses it can be put to).

The spaces indicate where there are no obvious links between paragraphs. Where there are no obvious links, the reader can assume that a new stage in the narrative is about to begin.

If we want to make sure that we are going to grasp the main points of the passage, these linking phrases help us to see how the text is put together. They help us to see where the main breaks in the text occur, and which paragraphs are linked to which ones. If you are looking for a specific point in the text that you want to make notes on, these paragraph linkers will help you see where the writer begins his point and where he ends it.

Paragraph linkers help you:
A to understand the general drift of a passage;
B to work out what are the main points of the passage;
C to see where a particular point made by the writer starts and ends.

Paragraph linkers help you to understand texts in another important way. They allow you to ask questions about paragraphs in the same way that you practised asking questions about the titles of books and chapters to check that you have understood them.

Look again at the linkers for the text on sugar cane.

Paragraph 2: 'Two conditions need to be fulfilled . . .'

You can ask yourself the question: 'What are the two conditions?'

If you scan through the paragraph and do not understand what the two conditions are by the end of it, then you can be sure you have not grasped the main point of the paragraph.

What are the two conditions? Write them down.

Paragraph 4: 'Another advantage . . .'

'Another' tells you that there has been (at least) one other advantage discussed already. You can ask two questions here:
(a) What was the advantage discussed in the last paragraph?
(b) What is the advantage discussed in *this* paragraph?

Answer both of these questions.

Paragraph 8

The linker here was 'the'. 'The' is used when a writer uses a word or a concept for a second time. So you can ask: What did the writer say about ligno-cellulose in the previous paragraph? Try to answer this question.

Now look at the following text, 'First It Was "Save the Whales," Now It's "Free the Dolphins"'.

Do the same things with the text as you did with the text on sugar cane.

This is quite a long text with many paragraphs. In fact, because it is so long, this exercise will concentrate on only the first two-thirds.

Try to decide how the text is constructed. How does each paragraph relate to the last?

EXERCISE 5.6

Write the linking words for each of the paragraphs. (The first two have been done for you.)

Para. 2   (No linking words)
Para. 3   The young man

EXERCISE 5.7

What questions can you ask yourself about the paragraph introducers in the paragraphs 3, 6, 8, 9, 11, 12, 15, 18, 19?

OPINION

FIRST IT WAS 'SAVE THE WHALES,' NOW IT'S 'FREE THE DOLPHINS'

BY SHANNON BROWNLEE

1 Jackie, a bottlenosed dolphin, lives in a small enclosure behind a restaurant on Longboat Key in Florida's Sarasota Bay. He spends the day in a seeming stupor, suspended in the murky water in a corner of his pen, his blowhole just above the surface. When customers come out to see him, he swims closer to the catwalk running along three sides of the enclosure, but he usually remains teasingly beyond the reach of the hands that seek to touch him.

2 At a little past 4 p.m. a lanky blond youth wearing reflector sunglasses saunters from the restaurant with a bucketful of Spanish mackerel. At his appearance Jackie perks up, swimming rapidly back and forth under der a pulpit that extends over the pen, and slaps the water with his tail. "Aw, he's just mad 'cause I'm ten minutes late," the young man tells the crowd gathered for the feeding. He leans over the railing of the pulpit to greet Jackie. "O.K., jerkface," he says.

3 The young man holds out a mackerel, shaking it slightly by the tail. The portly dolphin leaps from the water, exposing all of his nine feet and 600 pounds. At the zenith of his arc he grasps the fish in his toothy jaws, then falls back with a splash. Jackie chews on the mackerel half-heartedly before letting it drop to the bottom of the bay. After taking three more fish he refuses to budge, no matter how enticingly the young man waggles another. The young man shrugs. Shooing away some pelicans, he picks up his bucket and goes back inside.

4 There's nothing really wrong with Jackie, I'm told by my companion, a biologist who has studied bottlenosed dolphins in Sarasota Bay for nearly 17 years. He's just bored. And not surprisingly, considering his plight: he's cooped up with no comrades, has an indifferent keeper, and has nothing to do all day. I know what bottlenosed dolphins ought to be like. The bay teems with them—leaping, chasing fish, riding the bow waves of boats, scrapping with each other, having sex (a favorite activity among this species). Jackie must surely be miserable.

5 As we motor out into the bay to watch the wild dolphins, we wonder about the morality of denying such a boisterous, sociable mammal a life with his own kind. Indeed, should any marine mammals—dolphins, porpoises, whales, sea lions, seals, sea otters, *et al.*—be kept in captivity?

6 To an increasingly militant and well financed segment of the animal rights movement, the answer is unequivocally no. Activist

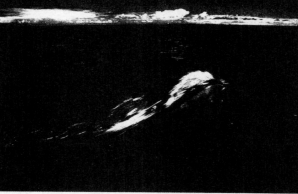

The exquisitely graceful spinner dolphin almost invariably dies in captivity.

groups include not only the much publicized Greenpeace, which has made saving whales a worldwide cause, but also the lesser known and even more radical Sea Shepherd, Project Jonah, and People for the Ethical Treatment of Animals. Many of them believe that keeping animals in a tank is an act of cruelty equivalent to keeping an innocent person in jail.

7 The people who work with marine mammals—aquarium and oceanarium curators, dolphin trainers, veterinarians, scientists—see the activities of animal rights groups as a threat to their professions, especially in view of the clout they've lately shown abroad. In response primarily to pressure from Greenpeace, legislation has been proposed in Britain and Australia to restrict dolphinariums or to close them entirely unless they institute sweeping—and expensive—reforms.

8 This turn of events wasn't entirely unexpected and isn't wholly unwarranted. In Australia and many European countries, captive marine animals have long been treated shabbily. In Clacton, England, for example, a young killer whale named Nemo lived in a ten-foot-deep swimming pool until he grew so large his owner (an American company) had to move him.

9 Captivity in the U.S. is much less grim, thanks in large part to the Marine Mammal Protection Act (MMPA), which passed in 1972 in the wake of the public outcry over whaling and the deaths of hundreds of thousands of dolphins each year in tuna nets. The MMPA regulates the treatment of both wild and captive marine mammals. Administered primarily by the National Marine Fisheries Service (NMFS, pronounced "nymphs" by those in the business), the act prohibits killing or harassing any marine mammal in U.S. waters (with certain exceptions: some native Alaskans, for instance, are permitted to kill a few bowhead whales each year). NMFS also closely monitors the conditions under which the more than 1,300 captive animals are kept. (Jackie, by the way, is another exception. He's a "grandfathered" animal, netted before the enactment of MMPA, which is why the restaurateur, a private owner, is allowed to keep him.)

10 The MMPA is an exemplary piece of conservation legislation, far stronger than the laws governing marine mammals in most other countries. Even so, many advocates of animal rights consider it woefully inadequate, and badly administered to boot.

11 They pose three fundamental objections to keeping these creatures captive. First, they charge that removing them from the wild

Animal rightists say keeping marine mammals is cruel. Scientists see extenuating circumstances

is endangering local populations, despite NMFS regulations. They concede that most cetacean species aren't in danger (the number caught for public display in the U.S. is actually quite small—a few dozen a year, at most) and nearly all pinnipeds (seals, walruses, sea lions) in oceanariums were born there, or were found sick or injured on beaches. But some species could be in jeopardy, particularly those whose numbers are easily depleted. In the late 1960s and early '70s so many young female killer whales were caught in the Pacific Northwest that the birth rates of wild pods are falling, as the remaining females have begun to reach the cetacean equivalent of menopause. (In reaction to early bungled captures in which a number of killer whales died, the state of Washington banished whale catchers from its waters.) Greenpeace advocates halting the capture of Commerson's dolphin, a South American species, because so many have been killed by crab fishermen in Chile, who cut them up and use them for bait.

12   Second, and more important, advocates of animal rights say the treatment of the captives is shockingly bad. Most of the animals kept in tanks, they contend, die at a younger age than those in the wild. Consider the fate of captive belugas, white Arctic whales sometimes called sea canaries for their high-pitched, melodious utterances. Of 31 netted for display in the U.S. and Canada since 1972, only 19 are still alive. Or the fate of captive killer whales: of 56 caught since 1965, 23 remain. Over a 15-year period one oceanarium collected 31 spinner dolphins, an exquisitely graceful, gregarious species that sports in Hawaiian waters. One was released. Twenty-nine died in captivity. The last dolphin, bereft of her companions, was finally released in 1983.

13   Third, say the protectionists, even if an animal survives, it's doomed to a pitiable existence. In their tanks or pens the captives become lethargic, indifferent, even neurotic, ritualistically repeating meaningless acts like swimming in tight circles or banging against the sides of their prisons. Their health deteriorates, and they gain weight. Chlorinated water irritates their skin and eyes. And, claim their defenders, normally loquacious dolphins become mute and their brains shrivel by as much as 30 per cent from lack of use.

14   Mammalogists point out that even though animal rights advocates like to cite scientific studies to support their alarmist claims, they've chosen increasingly to distance themselves from the methods and objectives of unbiased research, thus damaging their position. For example, the assertion that dolphins fall silent in captivity is wrong. They may emit sounds somewhat less often than dolphins do at sea, but dolphins in the wild have no choice but to communicate vocally, because they're often out of visual range of each other even during daylight. (One study, in fact, found that dolphins generally signal with body language if other dolphins are visible.)

15   Equally unsubstantiated is the claim that

dolphins' brains shrink in captivity. This finding is based largely on disputed comparisons of body-to-brain ratios between domestic and wild terrestrial mammals. A direct examination of the brain weights of captive and wild dolphins showed no significant difference.

16   Curators acknowledge that NMFS records of animals in captivity may not look good, but they say the raw numbers fail to tell the whole story. Most deaths occurred when oceanariums were making their first, often bumbling, attempts at caring for marine mammals, at a time when nobody knew how to do it. Those early losses sharply skewed the mortality statistics. For the most part, curators have abandoned trying to keep difficult species, such as the spinner dolphin, and survival rates are rising steadily for pinnipeds and some cetaceans (though not for all; few pilot whales, for example, have flourished in tanks—possibly, some scientists and trainers think, because they're such social creatures they can't live without their pod-mates).

17   **M**oreover, the animals are breeding in captivity. In 1983 a third of all captive bottlenosed dolphins were captive born, whereas in 1979 only a fifth were. At Sea World in Orlando, trainers and vets are coddling a baby killer whale born there in September 1985. Seals and sea lions are becoming so prolific that oceanariums don't know what to do with their offspring. Such fecundity, curators believe, demonstrates the quality of care, because unhappy and unhealthy mammals don't breed.

18   More difficult to refute is the contention of many activists that captive animals are wretched, especially in light of recent findings indicating that dolphins, whales, and pinnipeds are far more aware and intelligent than we suspected. Pinnipeds, for example, have extensive vocal repertoires with which they not only identify each other but also communicate their emotional states. Many cetaceans are adept vocal and behavioral mimics; simply by watching other members of their species, dolphins have been known to learn long and complicated show routines. And both bottlenosed dolphins and sea lions have shown they can respond to sentences transmitted to them by symbolic acoustic tones or by arm gestures, such as "Touch gate Frisbee,"—meaning "Touch the gate with the Frisbee"—a sentence they've never seen or heard before but understand because they know the meaning of each word (DISCOVER, Oct. 1985).

19   Such abilities, among many others, indicate that we're dealing with exceptionally brainy creatures, a fact that raises the disquieting possibility that we're causing them mental anguish. But how can we tell? Activists say the captives are despondent. Curators and trainers disagree. In truth, the reaction of the animals appears to vary enormously from species to species, and from individual to individual, but in the end nobody—not the animal rightists, not the scientists or trainers—can know how the animals really feel.

Hokey skits like this one do little to educate the public about sea lions.

OPINION

'*We'd do well to recognize that if animals have rights, it was we who conferred them*'

Anyway, the sensibilities of animals isn't the whole point. It's equally pertinent to ask how imprisoning them affects us. We too are diminished by it. The very word animal, deriving from *anima* (Latin for breath and soul), betrays the spiritual bond first felt by our ancestors, who depended on wild creatures for their existence. Captivity severs a strand of that ancient connection, which persists only in diluted form; it's there in the fables we read to our children and the exhilaration we feel upon hearing coyotes howl or glimpsing the flash of an elk's white rump through the trees.

Our relationship to animals shifted irretrievably when we stopped living among them and came to be responsible for them. As marine mammalogist Ken Norris has written, "I think we would do well to shunt aside the question of animal rights, recognizing that if there are rights we conferred them. Rather, we should realize that our growing wonder at the possible awareness of the other creatures on earth has a natural corollary: care."

But are we being good caretakers by holding a dolphin or a sea lion in a tank? Yes, if two conditions are met: that they're given the best treatment possible and, no less important, that they're displayed in a way that educates and informs us. Captive animals must be allowed to serve as ambassadors for their species.

This isn't a new idea. In the past decade most curators of zoos have come to consider conservation and informing the public their primary missions. However, many animal defenders believe that oceanarium curators trumpet education only to rationalize their true motive—making money.

As it happens, very few oceanariums are particularly profitable (the three Sea Worlds are notable exceptions), yet the opinion of animal rights groups is understandable. Until recently, oceanariums have always put on a gay public face, never letting on that any of their animals could take ill and die. How annoying—and insulting—it is to find out that the animal we see performing before us as "Shamu the Killer Whale" isn't the original Shamu, but one among many given that stage name over the years as their predecessors died.

A number of oceanariums, especially the commercially successful ones, are gaudy amusement parks in which marine mammals (and the public) are subjected to an intolerable degree of hokum. The animals have often been cast in comic roles—sea lions in ludicrous costumes, porpoises jumping through hoops, killer whales getting their teeth scrubbed with giant toothbrushes. Such shows do little to inform us of a beast's natural abilities.

To be fair, the shows have improved in the past five years. Most dolphins and whales no longer perform tricks in vapid skits (though sea lions and walruses still do). And even the dopiest performance did some good. When the first killer whale was put on public display, most people considered it a bloodthirsty carnivore that killed for sport—"savage sea cannibals," a 1954 TIME article called them. But after watching their trainers swim unmolested with them, the public changed its perception. Killer whales came

Sure, but which Shamu is it? The first, or the second, . . . or the sixth?

to be viewed as cute and lovable. For some people (especially some advocates of animal rights) these and other cetaceans are exalted almost as gods, far wiser and more peaceable than humans.

Certainly, a good portion of the more than 100 million people who visit zoological parks, aquariums, wildlife parks, and oceanariums each year is there solely to be entertained, but there's another component to our enchantment with these animals. They remind us that the planet is inhabited by creatures in many ways as remarkable as ourselves.

The desire to preserve the natural world begins with empathy, which can develop solely through direct contact. Such feelings can't be filtered through the media, print or film. Oceanariums, for all their razzmatazz, represent the only chance most of us will ever have to feel the quickening and expansion of our lives, to borrow John Muir's compelling phrase, that comes from viewing a sea lion, a walrus, or a whale. Indeed, the captives have a mission. It's largely up to them to stir compassion in the poor, bare, forked animal that wields the power to ensure their survival in the wild.

To anyone who has seen reflected in a dolphin's eye a deep and distant intelligence, the strident message of some extremists in the animal rights movement is profoundly disturbing. They would have these animals live completely apart from us. There would be no captives for scientific inquiry, and certainly none for public amusement. Oceanarium shows misinform, they say, and watching nature films is far superior to seeing these animals in tanks. Animal rights philosopher Tom Regan would even prohibit whale-watching tours, because they infringe upon the whales' right to privacy.

Carried to extremes, such views could eventually destroy the emotional and spiritual bonds with the natural world that form the basis for our environmental conscience.

Perhaps in a saner, gentler world we wouldn't need oceanariums and zoos. Perhaps the day will come when we won't have to imprison animals in order to hold on to some remnant of concern for them. But I doubt it. And with all the capital invested in oceanariums in this country, it's unlikely that the animal rights movement will succeed in getting them or research labs to release their animals any time soon. A much more sensible course for animal rightists would be to sit down with curators and scientists and discuss their practices—for the benefit of both the animals and ourselves.

Surely, we have much to learn about these marvelous creatures in our care, as I learned from Jackie, the bottlenosed dolphin. A number of the bars of his enclosure have rusted away, leaving holes wide enough for even fat old Jackie to swim through. And he knows where the holes are; once a manatee swam into his enclosure and he promptly chased it out. So why doesn't he leave to join the wild dolphins that cavort in Sarasota Bay? Is it fear? Is it an unwillingness to take risks after nearly a lifetime of captivity? For the moment, no one can tell what goes on in the mind of a dolphin. □

EXERCISE 5.8

Take one of your readings from a specialist subject, and try to do the same thing with it as you have just done with the texts in this unit. Choose the longest reading you can find!

UNIT 6

Writing Skills

PART 1

Introduction to Writing Skills

Whenever you are asked to write any assignment that is more than a few lines in length, you will either be asked to write something that *describes* a situation or an event, or you will be asked to *argue* about a particular point of view, saying either why it is correct or why it is wrong. In this unit, the first type of writing task will be called **descriptive**, and the second will be called **argumentative**.

- A descriptive approach is one in which you have to list important points. Your own point of view is often not required at all.
- An argumentative approach is one in which you have to state your own point of view, and to defend it by giving supporting arguments.

   If you want to do either of these tasks successfully, you will have to write a *logically organized essay*. This unit will show you how you can write such a logically organized essay, whether it is descriptive or argumentative. Logically organized essays rely on careful planning: for this reason a great deal of time will be spent on helping you to plan your essays carefully, so that your writing will be logical in its *thinking* and in its *presentation*.

Approaching Assignment Titles

Below is a list of the type of assignment titles that you are likely to be given as a student.
   Do they demand a descriptive or an argumentative approach?

A word of warning: some of these assignments could be either, depending on how you choose to approach them!

1 Explain, with examples, how the system of government works.
2 In Europe democracy is moving inevitably towards dictatorship. To what extent is this true of other parts of the world?
3 What is the difference between knowledge and belief?
4 Outline some of the things that led to the defeat of the Japanese at the end of the Second World War.

5 Compare development in Africa and in Melanesia.
6 What are the inequalities in the present education system?
7 With examples, discuss how rapid development can be harmful to subsistence societies.
8 Compare and contrast the education system of the USA and your own country.
9 What influence did the Greeks have on the ancient Romans?
10 Write a concise description of the role of the World Bank in development today.

Probably you will not have the *facts* to answer these assignments, but you should be able to see what kind of approach is required.

Understanding Assignment Titles

During your time as a student, you will be expected to write on a vast variety of topics; with them will come a bewildering range of instructions. The list below will help you interpret what the lecturer means. However, **if you are not sure what any assignment you are given is asking you to do, you must ask the teacher concerned.** Remember, he has set you the assignment to find out what you know about the subject—not to find out if you understand how to answer assignments.

1 **Account for**	Explain why X is as it is.
2 **Give an account of**	Give a statement of facts in sequence, or in report form.
3 **Analyse**	Describe the various parts of X and explain how they work together, or whether they work together. Give points for and against.
4 **Compare**	Describe the major similarities between two or more things.
5 **Contrast**	Describe the major differences between two or more things.
6 **Compare and contrast**	Describe first the major similarities, and then the major differences, between two or more things.
7 **Define**	Write a brief paragraph explaining the meaning of . . . If there is more than one thing to define, explain any similarities or differences.
8 **Describe**	Give a detailed account of . . .
9 **Discuss**	Write about the various opinions you have been reading about on the subject. Give points for and against and draw a conclusion from the points presented. It can also mean the same as 'Describe'.

10 **Elaborate on**	Write about a statement or a quotation that is part of the question. Explain the statement or quotation in more detail and then state your point of view concerning it.
11 **Evaluate**	Give an opinion supported by evidence on the worth or value of something.
12 **Evaluate the validity of (statement X)**	Same as 'Evaluate', but the statement X is probably not accurate in some way. You must explain what is wrong with the statement before going on to state your opinion.
13 **Examine**	Divide into parts and describe each part critically.
14 **Explain**	Write out in detail; make clearer; examine reasons and causes.
15 **Illustrate**	Use a figure, a diagram, or specific examples to make the meaning clear.
16 **Justify**	Give reasons for your conclusions or opinions.
17 **List**	Present a group of items in the required order without comment unless asked for.
18 **Outline**	Describe the essential parts only.
19 **Relate X to Y**	Show what the connections are: discuss the similarities and differences.
20 **Show**	Give reasons and causes.
21 **State**	Present clearly and concisely.
22 **Suggest**	Propose a theory and defend it by showing how it could work.
23 **Summarize**	Give the main points omitting details.
24 **Trace**	Follow the development from its starting point.

EXERCISE 6.1

Which of these demand a descriptive approach, and which demand an argumentative approach?

Group together under headings: **A** the instructions requiring an argumentative approach; **B** the instructions requiring a descriptive approach; and **A/B** those which could be both.

Deciding What to Put In and What to Leave Out

Many students have problems deciding what they should put into an essay, and what they should leave out. If you are writing an essay on, say 'The Parliamentary System of Australia', what should you explain in your essay, and what do you not need to explain?

The following questions may well cross your mind. Should you explain:
- What a parliament is?
- What is meant by a system?
- What 'Australia' is?
- Something about the history of parliaments?
- The British Parliamentary system?
- Who the present Prime Minister of Australia is?
- What a democracy is?
- What a vote is?

and so on.

How are you going to decide?

WHEN YOU WRITE, THINK ABOUT YOUR AUDIENCE.

There are *two* things you must take into account when you set about writing an essay.

1 Think about the reason you are writing the essay at all.

Why has your tutor asked you to write the essay?

The answer to this question is probably because he wants to see if you have understood the work he has been giving you—either in the form of lectures you have attended, or in books or handouts he has required you to read.

2 Have a specific reader in mind when you begin to write.

Apart from your tutor, who has actually set you the assignment, you need to have another, imaginary, 'reader' in mind. It is very difficult to write an explanation of something for a person whom you know is an expert in it already, and so you need to have another 'reader' who is not so expert.

Who should this reader be? Well, there are certain specific guidelines to follow.

When you write an essay, imagine that you are explaining something to someone who
- is intelligent enough to be one of your colleagues;
- has a reasonable amount of common sense;
- knows almost nothing about your subject.

If you follow this simple guideline, you will not fall into the trap of wasting time explaining things that any sensible person knows, while at the same time you will explain things about your subject that need to be explained.

The best way that you can make this system work is to imagine that a real person is going to read the essay—*not* to mark it, but to gain an understanding of what you are writing about. You may like to choose someone like an elder brother or sister, or your father or uncle. Someone you respect, but who hasn't had the benefit of attending the course you are doing at present.

If you imagine you are sending information to a real person, you will avoid many of the problems involved in deciding what to put in and what to leave out.

Look at the list of questions you asked yourself about the parliamentary system of Australia. Which questions would you need to answer if you were writing an assignment on this topic?

PART 2

Writing a Descriptive Essay

In this unit we shall be looking at how to write an essay that describes a situation, a problem or a process.

Any essay that is a description or explanation should contain

- **an introduction,**
- **the main body of the text,**
- **a conclusion.**

Before we look at each section in turn, one point needs to be made. To help you to quickly master the technique of writing a logically arranged descriptive essay, the instructions given throughout this unit are very precise, just as they will be with the argumentative essay. This may seem too inflexible to you at first, but you should not worry too much about it. Once you have mastered the techniques covered by this unit you will be able to adapt them to suit your own style.

You may find all this rather strange at first, but please try to persevere. It will help you to work out how to stick to the point, and it will make your written work much more 'logical' in its presentation.

The Introduction

To write a descriptive essay, it is helpful to begin by asking yourself some questions. **Do not include the questions in the text of your introduction**. The *answers* to them provide the material for your introductory paragraph.

The questions you must ask yourself when you are planning your introduction are:

1 Do I need to **define** any of the terms in the title?
2 Why is the topic I am writing about **important**?
3 How am I **limiting** my discussion?
4 Can I break up my task into a **number** of areas?

Look at an introductory paragraph below, and see how the answers to the questions help to construct a paragraph.

Topic: Outline some of the things that led to the fall of the Roman.

1 (Roman Empire; fall)	In its day, the Roman Empire was the most powerful pol the world. However, in the fourth century AD the Emp crumble, leaving chaos in its stead. It is worth inves reasons for the decline of the Roman Empire, for many oi
2 (modern-day relevance)	involved still influence modern-day societies. Of course the Roman Empire did not vanish overnight, never to be seen again. Rome itself continued to influence European politics for centuries afterwards.
3 (limit to loss of 'unified political empire')	However, there was a point when it ceased to be the centre of a unified political empire and it is the factors that led up to this point in time that will be discussed in this essay. There are, of course, many factors in-
4 (five reasons for fall)	volved, but in general there were five reasons leading to the fall of the Roman Empire.

A Detailed Look at Each of These Four Sections

1 What do I need to define?

You will need to explain some of the terms so that you can show the person marking your assignment that you have understood what you must talk about. Either you must **define a term** or you must **explain some important features of the term**. Remember the introduction to this unit has just shown you how to decide what you do *not* have to explain.

Here are some other examples of the first section of an introductory paragraph:

Topic: **Explain, with examples, the role of the defence force in border disputes.**

There are three arms of the defence force, the Army, the Navy and the Airforce. All three of these can be involved in border disputes, depending on the location of the border under dispute.

Topic: **Outline some of the problems of urbanization in *one* third-world country.**

Urbanization is the process whereby a settlement becomes a town in its own right, usually through a conscious decision of government.

Sometimes a dictionary definition is useful, but you must treat this particular technique with great care: usually you will have to highlight a particular aspect of the term you are defining, rather than its entire 'meaning'.

An example of this is if we take the first title in the exercise below; we would need to define 'curfew', but *only* the fact that stringent curfews prevent people from going out to shops, cinemas or to restaurants. There is little point in talking about problems with visiting friends during a curfew.

REMEMBER: Often you will need to define more than one term in a title.

EXERCISE 6.2

Look at the list of topics below:
(a) What do you think you would have to **define** in each topic?
(b) How would you define it? (Remember, you need to define only the necessary aspects.)

1 **Discuss the effects a curfew has on business interests in a city.**
2 **To what extent does sexual equality lead to social change?**
3 **Describe two processes for extracting steel from ore.**
4 **Explain how a compass works.**
5 **Outline some of the dangers of development.**

    Once you have done these, compare what you have written with your partner's work.

2 Why is the topic important?

Often, especially in an essay discussing a topic, you will need to explain a topic's importance, either in terms of its relevance today, or in terms of its relevance to the general study of the subject.

    Here are some examples:

Topic: **Describe with examples the role of the defence force in border disputes.**

A study of the defence force's role in border disputes is worth examining because it is a good example of the way that the armed forces take over policing in areas where the police have little control.

Topic: **Outline some of the problems of urbanization in *one* third–world country.**

Urbanization is a process that is world-wide, and so any problem that one particular country is having will have implications for any other country that is contemplating the same process with any of its settlements.

EXERCISE 6.3

a Now look at each of the five topics you dealt with in Exercise 6.2 and **decide which of them will need a sentence or two explaining why it is important to deal with the topic**.
    Are there any that you do *not* need to do this with?
b Next, look at each of the topics you have decided need a section on importance, and write one or two sentences for each one.

3 How am I limiting my discussion?

This is the place in your paragraph where you tell your reader just what area you will be discussing. No essay can deal with *all* the aspects of a topic, and so you should select what you consider to be the **central point**.

If the central point is not clear from the title of the assignment itself, then your lecturer's guidelines will often help.

You should give *one* reason why you have restricted yourself here. Examples:

Topic: **Describe, with examples, the role of the defence force in border disputes.**

As most disputes are land-based, this discussion will limit itself to examining the role of the Army.

Topic: **Outline some of the problems of urbanization in *one* third-world country.**

This discussion will limit itself to urbanization in Pakistan, for this country is the one where urbanization has proceeded at a faster rate than most.

EXERCISE 6.4

Look again at the five titles in Exercise 6.2, and write a short section describing **how you will limit your discussion** for each of the topics.

---

4 Can I break up the task into a number of parts?

This is an important section, for it tells you, the writer, how many paragraphs you will be writing. Each paragraph will be *one* of your numbered parts.

Note:

1 **You should always use words like 'major', or 'main' or 'most important'** or you will run the danger of saying that the *only* things to say are the ones you are saying (which is of course not true!).

2 **This sentence should contain many of the words from your topic.** It should be very similar to the topic, to remind the reader of the topic that you are writing about.

3 **You should not write out here what the areas are that you will be describing.** The rest of your essay does that!

Here are some examples:

Topic: **Describe, with examples, the role of the defence force in border disputes.**

Although the army becomes involved in many ways, there are really three main roles that the defence force in general, and the Army in particular, has in border disputes.

Topic: **Outline some of the problems of urbanization in *one* third-world country.**

There are four major problems that countries like Pakistan are having with urbanization.

EXERCISE 6.5

a Look at each of the titles in Exercise 6.2. **What areas would you choose to break your discussion into** (think of four or five areas). For instance, in number 1 you might choose different types of business.

b Write a section for each of the five topics, explaining that each can be broken up into four areas.

REMEMBER: At this stage you do not say *what* the areas are!

The rest of your essay will discuss the various areas, so why use up space setting them out here? If you do put them in, then you run the risk of making your essay boring to read.

A checklist for writing the introduction

The questions you must ask yourself when you are planning your introduction are:

1 Do I need to **define** any of the terms in the title?
  RESTRICT YOURSELF TO DEFINING THE CENTRAL POINT.
2 Why is the topic I am writing about **important**?
3 How am I **limiting** the discussion?
  GIVE ONE REASON WHY YOU ARE LIMITING YOUR DISCUSSION.
4 Can I break up my task into a **number** of areas?
  DO NOT SAY WHAT EACH AREA IS AT THIS STAGE.

Before you go on with the rest of the descriptive essay, it will be useful to practise writing introductions with some real material.

Resource materials for the descriptive essay

Look back to Unit 4: Reading Skills, and find the passage about Taiwan's fishing industry.

On the next few pages are some more articles from the same source about the fisheries industry in South-east Asia. In the course of this unit you will be asked to write a descriptive essay based on these materials. First you will be writing an introduction, and then the rest of a descriptive essay.

Use the skills you have been practising in the Reading Skills unit to gather information for your essays.

In the Reading Skills unit you were set the assignment, 'Current attempts at farming fish (aquaculture) in South-east Asia'

Let's set about actually doing this assignment.

You may find that the answers you wrote in the Reading Skills unit will help you here.

CHINA

The responsibility system has helped

By Nancy Langston in Peking

China's marine production still exceeds freshwater production but an intensive freshwater aquaculture programme with an emphasis on pond development is aiming to narrow the gap. The total catch for 1982 was 5.16 million tonnes — 3.6 million tonnes of seawater products and 1.5 million tonnes of freshwater goods. At a national seminar on fishing in 1983, it was reported that aquatic products averaged a 12.2% increase during 1978-82 compared with 6.9% in the two decades before 1978.

The fisheries programme was stepped up in 1979 and from 1980 annual increases from freshwater fishing have averaged about 10%. In the previous decade annual freshwater increases averaged 3-5%. Estimates for the 1983 freshwater catch project a 12% increase to 1.75 million tonnes.

The government attributes the dramatic increase to the responsibility system which was introduced in China's rural sector in 1979 and permits the private sale of produce after the state quota is filled. In the fishing industry, peasants sign contracts with communes as individual or collective contractors for tracts of the state-owned waters. Xinhua newsagency reported that by the end of 1983, China had 3 million households specialising in fish breeding. Although marine production has dwarfed freshwater production consistently for the past three decades, a United Nations report suggests that because of over-fishing and pollution, marine production may have reached a peak and will level off if not decline. The government, therefore, has turned to freshwater fisheries.

One reason for developing fish farms is the need to improve the nutritional status of China's billion-plus population. Available statistics from the late 1970s, admittedly dated, indicated a 5 kg fish consumption per capita which, according to UN figures, is one-third of the world average. Another reason for bolstering fish farming is that fish are export earners. Aquatic products according to Trade Department figures are the fifth largest commodity in terms of value. Although only about 5% of total production in 1981 and 1982 was exported, the value was Rmb 59.9 million (US$27.29 million) and Rmb 58.4 million respectively.

Of 20 million ha of fresh water available in the country at least 5 million ha are considered suitable for fish farming. According to the Ministry of Agriculture, Animal Husbandry and Fishery, only 60% of that 5 million is currently being utilised.

In 1982, aquaculture production of 1.2 million tonnes from 3 million ha had accounted for 75% of total freshwater production. Of this, freshwater ponds with an area of 910,000 ha contributed 863,590 tonnes. There have been steady increases in the average production per ha of pond surface which in 1982 reached 949 kgs per ha. In the sub-tropical southern province of Guangdong, there are reported yields of 3 tonnes per ha.

Heartened by impressive gains in fish-pond cultivation. the government plans to bring about 100.000 ha of marginal agricultural land under aquaculture production within the next five years. Two projects with this strategy in mind, to be conducted with assistance from the UN's World Food Programme to develop aquaculture in low-

Fishing under ice: for more export-earners. XINHUA

lying saline-alkaline areas. are in Zhejiang province and the municipality of Tianjin. The total cost of the Zhejiang project is US$18.9 million with the government absorbing 51% of the cost while the Tianjin project's price tag is US$25.3 million with government funding 66%.

The scope of the massive projects essentially is the same calling for the construction of fish ponds. nurseries and support services. If goals are achieved. the first-year yield from the ponds which in each area are a total of 1.066 ha will be 1.600 tonnes. At a sale price of 85 US cents a kg, total sales revenue from fish will be US$1.36 million. Fish farmers in Zhejiang are projected to end up with a net income of US$531.2. nearly a threefold increase in the current annual income in the area. Those in Tianjin will not make as much.

The World Food Programme currently has a fisheries-development project in Jiangsu province to beef up production in Hongze Lake and the five adjoining communes by expanding production ponds. nurseries and improving the support services. ∎

has been from marine areas. The declaration of the Philippines' exclusive economic zone covering marine waters extending 200 mis from its shores is expected to boost investment and trade potential in the local industry. However, the problem of poaching in Philippine fishing waters by foreign craft, particularly from Taiwan, is expected to remain despite the new Law of the Sea. The share of marine fishing in total production (estimated at some 76% in the early 1980s as against more than 90% until the late 1970s) is expected to continue falling. In 1978 a total of 2,132 commercial fishing vessels with a gross registered tons (grt) of 103,078 tons were registered. The vessels' sizes ranged from 5 grt to 1,000 grt, with 95% below 100 grt and about 81% below 50 grt.

Commercial fishermen have been asking for relief from certain taxes and licensing fees which they claim are discouraging further investments in the sector. But the Ministry of Natural Resources insists that the increase in the number of commercial fishing vessels and tonnage alone signified that investors were still willing to enter commercial fishing despite the levies. With the recent reorganisation of the Ministry of Agriculture and Food to equip it better for the thrust into massive agriculture-oriented economic programmes with huge financial assistance from the World Bank, the fisheries sector, now under its regulation, should benefit tremendously.

Aquaculture covers production from freshwater and brackish-water fishponds, lakes, rivers, reservoirs and more recently rice paddies. Advances have been noted particularly in the culture of milkfish and prawns which can be raised in the same environment, also known as polyculture. However, the now defunct Fishing Industry Development Council noted that this type of aquaculture was not yet widely practised in the Philippines "due to the extra capital and operational inputs required and the need for specialised technological practices." The council expressed optimism that polyculture would be pursued in earnest in the future, given the attractive profitability that it offers to fish farmers in terms of dual yields from only one fishpond area.

Of more immediate problems affecting the fisheries sector, the high cost of fuel appears to be the most serious and the industry has long been clamouring for rebates equivalent to the tax portion of the fuel retail prices. However, the government does not appear ready or able to grant the request. ◻

PHILIPPINES

Treading water with difficulty

By Joe Galang in Manila

Fishing is one of the many industries in the Philippines currently finding it increasingly difficult to keep its head above water in harsh economic weather. The crunch came after three devaluations of the peso against the United States dollar and a massive soaking up of excess liquidity in the financial system. This was necessitated by the government campaign to secure new foreign loans, but is choking the flow of funds to such sectors as the fishing industry.

Perhaps the most dramatic impact here has been made by the big increases in prices of petroleum products, normally comprising about 40-50% of the industry's operating costs. The proliferation of motorised fishing vessels among both commercial and small-scale fishermen has made the industry vulnerable to oil-price changes. Such factors are expected to depress further the industry which in recent years has already been suffering. For instance, the financial statements by the top five commercial fishing companies filed with the Securities and Exchange Commission show that higher revenues are no guarantee of profits.

Of the five — Frabelle Fishing Corp., RBL Fishing Corp., Mar Fishing Corp., Frabal Fishing and Ice Plant Corp. and RJL Martinez Fishing Corp. — three incurred aggregate losses of ₱36 million (US$2 million) which wiped out the combined profits of the other two, amounting to only ₱5.3 million. However, there is no lack of hope over long-term prospects. The fishing industry — contributing more than US$1 billion, or 4.5% of the country's gross national product, every year and accounting for 5% of the labour force — has total available resources far exceeding land-area resources.

Fish production has been growing at an average rate of 5.5% a year, according to the Ministry of Natural Resources. Estimated at some 1.2 million tonnes in 1973, fish catch had risen to about 1.9 million tonnes by 1983 and production is targeted to grow to about 2.6 million tonnes by 1990.

More than 75% of total production

Routine aquaculture: now to polyculture of milkfish and prawns, too.

EXERCISE 6.6

What are you going to put in your introduction?

First of all: Look quickly through the articles to gather the information you need to answer this topic.

Once you have done this, and you are ready to begin planning the assignment, look at the questions below, and write down your answers.

1 Do I need to **define** any of the terms in the title? If so, which ones? How should they be defined?
2 Why is the topic I'm writing about **important**?
3 How am I **limiting** my discussion?
4 Can I break up my task into a **number** of aspects? If so, how many?

List the aspects you will be discussing in the essay. Remember: the number of aspects you will be discussing must correspond with the number you wrote in (4) above.

Look at the suggestions below. Are they the same as yours? Compare them with your own and decide which is better.

1 Aquaculture   Farming captive fish, usually in ponds.

Current   Since 1975 (because all the data available is from 1975 onwards).

Do *not* write 'because that is all the information in the article'. It sounds as if you were too lazy to read any further.

2 Fish stocks are becoming lower on a world-wide basis, and fish farming is the only way to ensure that there will be enough fish in the future.

3 To Taiwan, the Philippines and China (because that is all the information available in the articles). This is *not* a good reason to include in your essay because it gives the impression you have been lazy. A good reason you might write would be: 'Because they are reputedly the most successful.'

4 Three countries (because these fall into three geographical areas).
The three aspects are: Taiwan, China, the Philippines.

EXERCISE 6.7

Now put all this information together into a single paragraph. Don't forget that the four sections will need to be linked together with suitable phrases!

The Main Body of the Essay

You finished your introduction with a sentence something like this:

'Although most of the South-east Asian region is involved in aquaculture, it is these three countries that are having the most success in attempting to farm fish in South East Asia.'

Each of your following paragraphs should take **one country in turn**.

Each paragraph:
1 Begins with a restatement of the last sentence of your Introduction.
2 States your information in detail.
3 Ends with an example. .
  Look at this example:

1 (first reason)	The first major reason for the fall of the Roman Empire was a financial one. As Roberts (1980:286) says, 'the state apparatus in the West gradually seized up after the recovery of the 4th century'. A lack of conquests meant that the
2 (no money for army)	Roman state had no way of financing its enormous army apart from taxing its citizens heavily. So high were the taxes that the majority of the wealthy gave up trying to produce foodstuff for trade, and instead concentrated on becoming self-sufficient. As trade declined, so did the finances to support the army, and before long the huge numbers of highly trained men were re-
3 (example, army in Gaul)	placed by a poorly trained, ill-equipped force. The army in Gaul, for example, consisted mainly of local peasants, with only a handful of Roman citizens to control them. As soon as an army like this meets opposition, it simply melts away.

Now look at your essay on aquaculture.

Remember, each paragraph should deal with one of the three countries, and repeat some of the words of the last sentence of your introduction. You will need to write *three* paragraphs, as you have limited yourself to China, Taiwan and the Philippines.

How will you begin each one?

EXERCISE 6.8

What will you **describe** in each paragraph?
  Scan for the information you require in each of the texts in turn, and write some notes for each of the countries.
REMEMBER: Your **aim** is to read for information on aquaculture only.
  Now look at your notes. What would you put for an **example** of the extent to which each country is committed to aquaculture?
  Check with your partner. Do you both have the same? If they are different, which is better?

EXERCISE 6.9

Now write up the three paragraphs of your essay on aquaculture.

The Conclusion

The conclusion to a descriptive essay should not be a long one.
  You can do the following:
A Write about the future implications of what you have described.

or

B Write about the influence of what you have described on wider issues.

or

C Suggest how the situation could be improved in some way.

DO NOT JUST REPEAT WHAT YOU WROTE IN THE INTRODUCTION.

DO NOT JUST RESTATE THE MAIN POINTS OF EACH PARAGRAPH.

Look at this conclusion to the essay on *The Fall of the Roman Empire*:

There were, then, many reasons why the Roman Empire fell. As the empire crumbled, it became divided into the two centres of Rome and Constantinople. The resulting rivalry meant that the Arab forces were able to gain much more ground in Europe and North Africa than they might otherwise have done. In the long term this was perhaps an advantage to European culture as a whole, for it exposed Europe to Arab philosophy and science: both of which were in many ways far superior to those in Europe at the time.

What kind of conclusion is this? Write down what the **main idea** of the conclusion is. Which of the three suggested types of conclusion is this one?

Now look at your essay on Aquaculture. What kind of conclusion could you write?

Write one sentence which will sum up what you are going to say in your conclusion, and compare it with your partner's. Which is better?

EXERCISE 6.10

Now write a complete concluding paragraph for your essay on aquaculture.

EXERCISE 6.11

Assignment

Look again at the texts on fishing, and write the following essay, using the technique discussed above:

'In about 300 words, compare the fishing industries of Taiwan and the Philippines.'

REMEMBER: Before you read the articles again, **decide on your purpose**.

Here is a checklist to help you lay out your assignment properly.

The descriptive essay

Introduction

When you write your introduction, ask the following questions:

1 Do I need to define any of the terms in the title?

2 Why is the topic I am writing about important?
3 How can I limit my discussion?
4 Can I break up my task into a number of areas?

Main body of the essay

Each paragraph:
- begins with a restatement of the last sentence of your Introduction;
- states your information in detail;
- ends with an example.

The conclusion

You can do the following things:
Write about the future implications of what you have described.
or
Write about the influence of what you have described on wider issues.
or
Suggest how the situation could be improved in some way.

Using Graphs and Tables in an Essay

Often the most useful sources of numerical information appear in your readings in the form of either **graphs** or **tables**.

This unit will help you to put the information from graphs and tables properly into your assignments.

Presumably you will have had some practice in using graphs and tables previously—probably in mathematics lessons.

Many students are quite able to understand graphs and tables, but have great difficulty in knowing what to write about them when they do include them in an assignment. This problem is particularly difficult because often the graph or table was written for one purpose which may well be different from you own: you may only want to use *some* of the information, and not all of it.

When you use a graph, you must:
1 only extract what is relevant to *your purpose*;
2 show the person marking your assignment that *you are in control of the information*.

Using a graph

You have been given the following assignment: 'Describe the differences between the populations of modern-day industrial societies and those of pre-industrial ones.'

You have found four graphs of population structures for Sweden in 1978, Sweden in 1751, Venezuela in 1977 and the Ivory Coast in 1975. They deal with modern industrialized Sweden, Sweden before industrialization, and two developing countries, so they should be exactly what you need.

How do you go about using them?

If you think back to Unit 4: Reading Skills, you will remember that it suggested that you work out what information you are looking for *before* you begin reading a text. Graphs and tables are no different.

Once you have **defined your purpose** (which will arise from the topic of your assignment), you should approach the task of using them by following three steps:

Step 1. Make sure you understand the graph.

Step 2. Describe the situation presented by the graph or table from ONE point of view only (i.e. one country, or one product, or one date).

Step 3. Compare other points of view in terms of the situation you have described in step 2.

Look at the population graphs below:

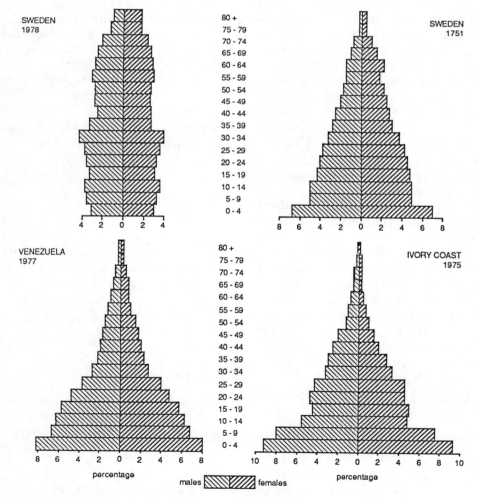

The population structure of Sweden in 1978 and 1751 and of Venezuela in 1977 and Ivory Coast in 1975
Source: J. P. Cole, 1983, *Geography of World Affairs*, Figure 3.5.

Step 1 Understanding the graph

The first thing that you must do when you approach any graph or table is to make sure you know what the *vertical axis* and the *horizontal axis* are describing. Usually the two axes are sequences of numbers of some kind: and before you can understand the graph, you must be sure of the meaning of the numbers. Look at the four graphs of population structure. All four graphs have the same axes. Write down what the two axes of the graphs are.

Once you are sure you have understood the axes, you can look at the other special features of the graph.

In each of these graphs there are two kinds of shading: the one to the left of the vertical axis is lighter than the one to the right. What do the different kinds of shading mean?

Step 2 Describing the situation from one point of view

As has been said many times so far in this course, before you begin any reading or writing task, **you must have your purpose clear in your mind**. In the case of a graph or table, you must decide what it is you need to describe. This of course depends on your assignment and the role the graph or table will play in your argument.

In this example you are looking for general information on population structure in societies that are industrialized and societies that are not.

Let us decide what information you need.

If you are looking for information on population structure, what sort of things would you be looking for? Write out a **question** for each of the following:
1 About the majority of the population.
2 About old people.
3 About numbers of old men and women.
4 About comparing young and old.

If you look at the graph, you will see that you can give two kinds of answers: one relying on the five-year blocks chosen by the person compiling the statistics, and another kind of answer relying on your adding together some of these blocks to make a larger block.

Did you get something like this?
1 What age group makes up the majority of the population?
2 How many people are there over retirement age (65 and over)?
3 Are there as many old men as there are old women?
4 Are there more children than old people?

Your answer to 1, if you rely on the five-year blocks, would be

1 The largest proportion of the population is in the 30–34 age range (8% are in this group: 4% men, 4% women).

Your answers to 2 and 3, however, would involve you in forming a larger block, and so you would probably answer:

2 16% of the population is over 65.
3 There are ten women for every seven men over the age of 65, but over 75 there are two women for every man.

The most relevant part of this graph, and therefore the one you will almost certainly want to describe, is the section that deals with the 0 to 4-year-olds, for there are so few children of that age group in the Swedish chart compared to the other charts. For this reason you will need to describe both a five-year block (the 0 to 4-year-olds, and the 5 to 9-year-olds) and a larger one (the 0 to 9-year-olds—a group formed by adding the percentages in each of the five-year blocks together). You may well want to write something like this:

4 About 13% of the population is under 10 years of age, and, of these, only 6% of the population is in the 0 to 4-year-old group.

Step 3 Comparing other points of view in terms of the situation described in Step 2

EXERCISE 6.12

Now look at graph 2, which describes the population of Sweden in 1751. Look at the four questions we asked about the first graph, and try to answer them with reference to this second graph:
1 What age group makes up the majority of the population?
2 How many people are over retirement age (65 and above)?
3 Are there as many old men as there are old women?
4 Are there more children than old people?

Look at what you have written about this graph and what was written about the first graph of Sweden in 1978. Can you make any direct comparisons? Write out *three* comparisons you can make. The areas of discussion have been indicated below to help you.

1 Largest percentage of the population
   1978
   1751
2 Number of old people (60+)
   1978
   1951
3 Men versus women
   1978
   1951

EXERCISE 6.13

Now, write out your comparison in the form of a short paragraph, and try to draw some conclusions, if you can.

Begin by describing the situation in present-day Sweden, and then go on to *compare* present-day Sweden with the data from 200 years earlier.

Look at the end of this section for a suggestion of how you might have written your paragraph.

EXERCISE 6.14

Now look at the other graphs to help you find more facts to use in the assignment.

Look at the other two population graphs, one for Venezuela and one for the Ivory Coast. Both of these are pre-industrialized societies, and so they should be suitable for use in your discussion.

Write a short paragraph comparing these two graphs, using the same technique as before. Describe the first graph, and then describe the *same features* of the second in such a way that you draw comparisons. Finally, write some conclusions.

Next, look at the four graphs below. You have been set the essay: 'UK's main sources of energy in the years 1970 to 1980'.

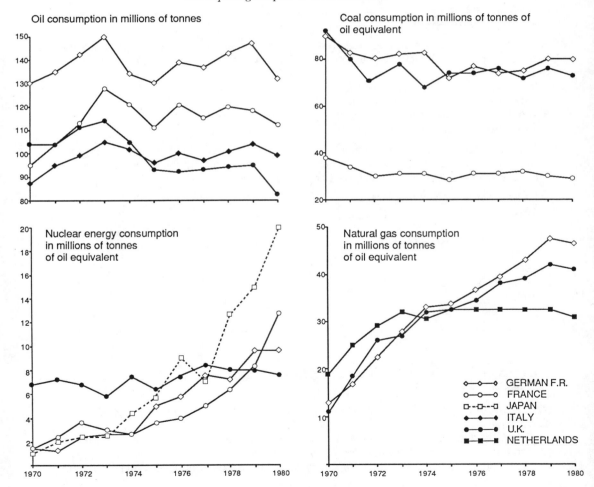

Developed regions poor in natural resources

Consumption of major types of energy in selected West European countries in the 1970s
Source: J. P. Cole, 1983, *Geography of World Affairs*, Figure 9.7.

These graphs look a little different from the last ones, but in fact you can still do exactly the same things with them.

In the first example we took the most recent statistics as a starting point, and then described the other graphs in terms of the first one. What would be the most useful starting point to deal with these graphs?

There is no right answer to this! The best answer is the one that suits your own purpose. Here it might perhaps be the consumption of *one* of the sources of energy over the past ten years. Try doing it.

EXERCISE 6.15

Write a short paragraph describing the consumption of *one* of the sources of energy.
 Your discussion should cover the following points:

1 **Definition** of the four main sources of energy.

2 State some of the facts and figures for one of the sources that is becoming **less important** (a falling curve).

3 Compare this with a source of energy that is becoming **more important** (a rising curve).

4 Draw any **conclusions** you can.

 It will be easier if you base your discussion on five-year blocks.

Using tables in your written work

Tables are often very daunting things, as they usually contain long lists of numbers laid out in a very unappealing way. However, they are just as useful as graphs, and should be studied carefully when you are looking for facts and figures to back up a point.

 Look at Table 1 (on p. 136) describing the ten largest producers of basic foodstuffs in 1979.

1 The ten countries are pretty obvious, but what do the numbers mean? Look at the top line and try to work out what A and B represent.

2 Have you got it? The graph or table will always give you the information **somewhere**.

3 You will have noticed that there are six lists of country names. Why is this? Are they the same countries each time?

 Now try to use this information in the assignment, 'Compare the agricultural production of the USSR and the USA in recent years'.

 What can you say about the USSR's production of foodstuff in 1979:
(a) in terms of variety of foodstuffs?
(b) in terms of millions of tons produced?

 How does this compare with the USA's production of foodstuff in the same year?

Table 1 *The ten largest producers of six basic food items in millions of tonnes in 1979*

Country	Wheat A	B	Country	Maize A	B	Country	Rice, paddy A	B
1 USSR	90.1	21.2	1 USA	197.2	50.1	1 China	143.4	36.0
2 China	60.0	14.1	2 China	40.6	10.3	2 India	69.0	17.3
3 USA	58.3	13.7	3 Brazil	16.3	4.1	3 Indonesia	26.4	6.6
4 India	35.0	8.2	4 Romania	12.4	3.1	4 Bangladesh	19.4	4.9
5 France	19.4	4.6	5 France	10.3	2.6	5 Thailand	15.6	3.9
6 Canada	17.7	4.2	6 Yugoslavia	10.1	2.6	6 Japan	15.6	3.9
7 Turkey	17.6	4.1	7 Mexico	9.3	2.4	7 Viet Nam	10.5	2.6
8 Australia	16.1	3.8	8 Argentina	8.7	2.2	8 Burma	10.0	2.5
9 Pakistan	9.9	2.3	9 USSR	8.4	2.1	9 Korean R	8.1	2.0
10 Italy	9.1	2.1	10 South Africa	8.2	2.1	10 Brazil	7.6	1.9
World	425(100%)	78%	World	394(100%)	82%	World	398(100%)	82%

Country	Barley A	B	Country	Potatoes A	B	Country	Raw Sugar (centrifugal) A	B
1 USSR	46.0	26.7	1 USSR	90.3	31.7	1 Cuba	8.0	9.0
2 China	19.5	11.3	2 Poland	49.6	17.4	2 USSR	7.6	8.5
3 France	11.2	6.5	3 USA	15.8	5.5	3 Brazil	7.0	7.9
4 UK	9.6	5.6	4 China	14.0	4.9	4 India	6.4	7.2
5 Canada	8.5	4.9	5 German DR	12.5	4.4	5 USA	5.1	5.7
6 USA	8.2	4.8	6 India	10.0	3.5	6 France	4.2	4.7
7 German FR	8.2	4.8	7 German FR	8.7	3.1	7 China	3.6	4.0
8 Denmark	6.7	3.9	8 France	7.1	2.5	8 German FR	3.3	3.7
9 Spain	6.2	3.6	9 UK	6.5	2.3	9 Mexico	3.1	3.5
10 Turkey	5.2	3.0	10 Netherlands	6.3	2.2	10 Australia	3.0	3.4
World	172(100%)	75%	World	285(100%)	78%	World	88.9(100%)	58%

Source: FAOPY 79 Tables 10, 13, 11, 12, 19, 60
A = total production in millions of tonnes; B = percentage of world total

Table 2 *The five largest producers of non-cereal crops and of three beverages in thousands of tonnes in 1979*

Country	Soybeans A	B	Country	Groundnuts A	B	Country	Palm oil A	B
USA	61 700	65.5.	India	5 800	30.2	Malaysia	2180	48.1
China	13 100	13.9	China	2 900	15.1	Nigeria	680	15.0
Brazil	10 000	10.6	USA	1 800	9.4	Indonesia	610	13.5
Argentina	3 700	3.9	Sudan	1 100	5.7	China	180	4.0
Mexico	700	0.7	Senegal	1 000	5.2	Zaire	170	3.8
World	94 200(100%)	95%	World	19 200(100%)	66%	World	4530(100%)	84%

Country	Coffee A	B	Country	Cocoa beans A	B	Country	Tea A	B
Brazil	1300	26.2	Ivory Coast	350	22.1	India	550	30.2
Colombia	760	15.3	Brazil	309	19.5	China	303	16.6
Ivory Coast	280	5.6	Ghana	270	17.0	Sri Lanka	210	11.5
Indonesia	270	5.4	Nigeria	180	11.4	Turkey	117	6.4
Mexico	230	4.6	Cameroon	115	7.3	Japan	106	5.8
World	4970(100%)	57%	World	1585(100%)	77%	World	1821(100%)	71%

Sources: FAOPY 79 Tables 28, 29, 39, 69, 70, 187

A = total production; *B* = percentage world total

Source: J. P. Cole, 1983, *Geography of World Affairs*, Tables 5.1, 5.2.

EXERCISE 6.16

Write a short paragraph comparing the USA and the USSR, following the same plan as you have been following in this unit.
1 Make sure that you understand the graph.
2 State some of the facts and figures for one country (USSR?).
3 Compare the other country's production with the first one by referring back to the facts and figures you described in 2.

EXERCISE 6.17

Assignment

Look at Table 2, the five largest producers of non-cereal crops and of three beverages in thousands of tonnes in 1979.

Write a short paragraph describing Brazil's production of beverages in relation to the rest of the world's production.

Answer to Exercise 6.13

Did you write something like this?

According to Cole (1983:45), Sweden's population in 1978 was very different from its population in 1751, before it became an industrialized nation. In 1978 16% of the population was over the age of 65, while only 13% were under the age of 10. The figures are presented in five-year blocks, and if one looks at these, the data is very interesting. The largest single group was the 30 to 35-year-olds, who made up 8% of the population, while the 0 to 4-year-olds only made up about 6%. About 6% of the population was over the age of 70, and of these there were twice as many women as men. This ratio of aged women to aged men is about the only similarity with the population structure of pre-industrial Sweden. In 1751 there was only a third as many people alive over 65 (5%), whereas there were over twice as many people under the age of 10 (28%). In fact the largest single age group was the 0 to 4-year-olds, who made up 14% of the population. There were far fewer people over the age of 70: a sixth, in fact (1%). Overall, it seems that Sweden in the 1970s had many more old people and far fewer children than pre-industrialized Sweden.

PART 3

Writing an Argumentative Essay

Defending Your Point of View

In this part of the unit you will be looking at how to write an essay that **puts forward one point of view** and tries to **defend** that point of view.

Defending a point of view is perhaps the most frequently used *extended* writing exercise in academic life. Most of the long essays you will be asked to write will be argumentative ones. So it is worth spending a little time trying to get this technique right.

Why do teachers and lecturers expect one to do this so often?

The reason is simple. The argumentative essay is a very useful test of a student's ability to think **logically**.

To write a good argumentative essay, your approach to the topic must be logical from the beginning. A logical argument is the sign of a clear thinker. A muddled argument is the sign of muddled thinking.

A special note: There are many ways of writing an argumentative essay, and none of them are 'wrong'. However, this unit will suggest one method of writing an argumentative essay that is used by many professional academics in their own work. If you can master this technique it will help you get through many of the books and articles that you will read throughout the rest of your academic career.

To help you master this technique quickly, the instructions given are very precise, just as they were with the descriptive essay. Please try to follow the technique suggested. Remember, once you have mastered the technique you will be able to adapt it to suit your own style.

The technique suggested here will help you work out how to stick to the point, and it will make your arguments much more logical in their presentation.

Essay Topics

The following essay topics are to help you do the exercises that follow. In this unit you will be told when to use them, and how to use them. The exercises in the unit will help you to gradually build up a detailed plan of an argumentative essay on each of the topics below.

The topics are here as an aid to your inspiration. Your tutor may substitute other titles, perhaps more suited to your major subjects.

Write only what you are told to, when you are told to!

1 **Crime**
2 **City life**
3 **Should smoking be made illegal?**
4 **Religion and the modern world**
5 **The role of universities**
6 **Nuclear energy**
7 **Divorce**
8 **Sexual equality**
9 **Traffic**
10 **Is money really the root of all evil?**
11 **Natural resources**
12 **Development**
13 **Television**
14 **Education: for employment or for the 'whole' man?**
15 **Politicians**

The Introduction

An argumentative essay is usually a discussion of a topic, giving reasons why the writer holds a particular point of view. Most academic papers or articles are laid out in such a way that the introduction sets out the problem, and the paragraphs that follow give supporting arguments for the writer's point of view.

If you look carefully at most professionally written academic articles, you wil find that the introduction is laid out more or less like this:

1 A section relating the topic to the reader's own experience (you may need one or more sentences for this).
2 A question that sets out the problem behind the topic (*one* sentence only).
3 A section showing why people who disagree with the writer are likely to hold their opinion (you may need one or more sentences for this).
4 A sentence that sets out your own opinion on the topic (one sentence only).

Let us look at each of these components as they actually occur in an introduction. In the following paragraph identify the four parts of the introduction.

THE ECONOMICS OF OIL PRICING

In his article on the use of the 'oil weapon' in the 1970s, H. Brown (1984:23) suggests that the main reason for the rapid increase in oil prices was the cost of the Arab–Israeli wars. But was that really the main reason behind the enormous price increases at that time? Brown argues that the price rises were the only way of providing cash to replenish the huge amount of weapons lost by the Arabs in the wars. There are, however, other far more important reasons behind the price increases at that time than a mere shortage of cash.

1 The section relating the topic to the reader's own experience

Papers or essays are nearly always written for a reason. Often a topic is written about because of recent publicity in the newspapers, or because someone in a previous academic journal has put forward a point of view that the writer of a present article does not agree with.

Most professional writers will try to begin their article or paper by reminding their readers of the recent event or discussion. This is for a very good reason. It says to the reader: 'This is something you will be interested in. It is going to discuss something you have been thinking about recently.' It is a technique worth following in your own writing: an essay that starts by arousing the tutor's interest is likely to gain more marks than one which doesn't.

Often you will need to write several sentences to describe the recent event or discussion, but sometimes only one sentence can be enough. Here are some examples.

The recent troubles in the Middle East have been widely reported in the world's press.

In last week's daily papers there was a great deal of coverage given to a case of child beating. The parents, it seemed, were blaming their cramped housing on their sudden loss of control.

In the last year there have been over five hundred violations of air traffic rules in the United States.

What essay topics do you think each of these is introducing?

The more DATES, FACTS AND FIGURES you can give in your introductory section, the better!

EXERCISE 6.18

Look at the topics listed on page 139, and write out some introductory sentences for the first *five* of the topics.

2 A question that sets out the problem behind the topic

We shall call this the **issue**.

This is perhaps the most important part of your essay, because it helps to make perfectly clear what the essay is actually discussing.

Look at the paragraph below, and see how the issue helps to define the theme of the essay.

FOOTBALL VIOLENCE

1   In a recent article about the role of the police in the handling of football crowds,
J. Hanson suggested that police should be armed with 2-metre clubs with spikes on
2   the end (Hanson, 1984:27). **Is arming the police really the right way to go**
3   **about solving law and order problems at sports events?** Hanson suggests that
giving the police weapons is necessary because the only way to meet violence is with
4   violence. There are, however, more sensible ways of dealing with law and order at
sports events.

(The numbers on the left refer to the four parts of the paragraph mentioned
above; the *issue* is number 2.)

The issue defines what the discussion is going to be about. The essay is not
going to discuss whether the clubs should be two metres or three metres long:
it is not going to discuss whether football should be banned: it is not going to
discuss whether there is, in fact, violence at sports events.

> What *is* it going to discuss? Write out what you think it is.

By putting the issue right at the beginning, several things are achieved:
(a) The **reader** is told from the beginning what the writer will be arguing
about: what aspect of the problem is going to be discussed.
(b) Often the writing of an issue shows a **writer** what he 'really' wants to
write about. Putting down the issue helps to clarify the writer's own mind.
(c) The **writer** is forced to stick to *one* main point in the essay, and because of
that he or she is forced to decide what that one main point really is. If the
writer in the example above had actually wanted to discuss what arms the
police should carry, then the issue would have had to be revised to reflect
that.

If the writer had wanted to discuss **what arms the police should be
given**, the issue would have had to be rewritten to read something like this:
'Are these really the kind of arms the police should carry?'

Often poor essays can be traced back to 'lame issues'. A lame issue is one
that does not have two sides to it.

Here are some examples of lame issues:

Is theft a crime?

Should children do what their parents tell them?

Is the world round?

Should we obey the traffic rules?

Are women legally equal to men?

Is violence a bad thing?

For instance: 'Is theft a crime?' is a lame issue because the word 'theft'
means 'to take something illegally': crime is illegal, so the question is circular—
'is an illegal act illegal?'

You could change this to make a useful issue by rewriting it as 'Can one
ever justify taking other people's property?'

This is a good issue, because there are two sides:

1 YES—because if one's child is starving it is right to take food to survive.
2 NO—because taking other people's property is theft, and theft is a crime.

EXERCISE 6.19

Why are the others bad issues? Try to change them so that they become usable ones. Write out your answers to each question.

1 *Should children do what their parents tell them?*
   ● Why is it lame?
   ● What is your revised issue?

2 *Is the world round?*
   ● Why is it lame?
   ● What is your revised issue?

3 *Should we obey the traffic rules?*
   ● Why is it lame?
   ● What is your revised issue?

4 *Are women legally equal to men?*
   ● Why is it lame?
   ● What is your revised issue?

5 *Is violence a bad thing?*
   ● Why is it lame?
   ● What is your revised issue?

EXERCISE 6.20

Look at the list of topics on page 139. You have already written opening sentences for the first *five* topics in Exercise 6.18. Now write **issues** for these first five topics.

REMEMBER: Each issue should be in the form of a **question**.

Once you are happy with your opening sentences and issues, write each of the first five topics at the top of a fresh side of paper, and beneath each one write your introduction and your issue, as if you are beginning an essay. Later you will be writing more on these sheets, so *keep them carefully!*

Note: Some of the topics are phrased as questions. **Don't be tempted to change these questions!** They are already the issues you should be discussing.

3 A statement of why some people disagree with the writer, and are likely to hold that opinion

If you have a good issue, you will have an argument that has two sides to it. A good issue is one where you could imagine two people coming to blows over it!

When you write a sentence that shows the opposite side to your own point of view you are doing several things:

(a) You are telling the reader, who may in fact already have the opposite point of view to you about your issue, that the opposing argument does have some strong arguments to support it.

(b) You are making sure that your issue does really have two sides to it. If you can't find a good reason why someone should hold the opposite point of view to you, then you haven't got a good issue!

Notice how the third sentence in the paragraph quoted on page 141 about football violence gives *one* reason only why the man with a different point of view to the writer holds his opinion.

Don't give more than one support for the other argument. It weakens your own.

Introduce the opposing argument with a phrase like these:

> Some people maintain . . .
>
> It can be argued that . . .
>
> It might be said that . . .

Notice that these introducers contain words like 'can', 'might' and so on, making the facts in the sentence that follows seem not very certain.

Notice the difference between:

1 **Students are lazy people.**

(This sounds like a fact; the speaker is very definite about it. It is the speaker's *own* opinion.)

2 **It might be said that students are lazy people.**

(This sounds as if the speaker is doubtful about the fact expressed. The speaker does *not* agree with this opinion.)

When you are expressing an opinion you do not agree with, you should use sentences like the **second** one.

EXERCISE 6.21

Can you think of any more introductory phrases like the ones just given for sentences containing an opinion you do not agree with? Write them down.

Try to use these phrases in the exercises that follow.

EXERCISE 6.22

So far you have written opening sentences and an issue for each of the first five topics. For this exercise look at the issues you wrote for Exercise 6.20, and write a sentence for each of these five topics that illustrates **a point of view different from the one that you will be taking**.

REMEMBER: Begin with an introductory phrase, and include *one* reason only why the point of view could be considered valid.

4 A statement that sets out the writer's own opinion on the topic

We shall call this the **main idea statement**, or MIS for short.

Your main idea statement tells the reader what you, the writer, think about the issue. **The MIS is the *answer* to the *question* posed by the *issue*.**

Note that you *do not write any reasons* why you hold this opinion. The rest of your essay is giving all the reasons, so **you do not write them in the introduction**. Most students find it very hard to write a MIS without giving any reasons—there is no need to do this, as you are going to discuss them at length in the paragraphs to come.

Introduce your MIS with phrases like this:

> However, it is clear that. . .
>
> There are many reasons why. . .

Because this is your own opinion, the one you believe in, your MIS should begin with a introducer that makes your point of view seem very certain—almost a fact. So you must make your sentence sound very definite. Avoid words like 'can' or 'might'. Use 'is' or 'are' and add perhaps phrases like 'of course', 'certainly'.

EXERCISE 6.23

What other introductory phrases for your MIS can you think of? Write them down.

Try to use these introducers in the exercises that follow.

EXERCISE 6.24

Look again at Exercise 6.20, where you wrote issues for each of the first five topics on the essay topics page. Write down the **topic**, the **issue**, and a **main idea statement** for each of the five topics.

Compare your issues with your neighbour's. Do you agree that he has written good issues? Are there any 'lame issues'? What about the main idea statements that your partner has written for each of the five topics. Do they really refer to the issues?

Once you are happy with what you have written, go to the five sheets of paper where you wrote the topic, the introduction and the issue for the first five topics, and complete your introductory paragraphs by adding the *counter-argument* and the *main idea statement* to each.

REMEMBER: You are writing the introductory paragraph for five essays: so all four sections should be written as **one paragraph** for each essay.

EXERCISE 6.25

We have now covered all four parts of the introductory paragraph. Look at the list of statements below, and decide whether they are:

A Topics
B Issues
C Counter arguments
D Main idea statements
E Lame issues

Write them out with A, B, C, D or E beside them.

1 Should the law on theft be changed?
2 The law on theft should be changed.

3 Examinations should be abolished.
4 Police are unnecessary because they aren't reducing crime.
5 Are people basically honest?
6 Traffic problems
7 Moslems make better human beings than Christians.
8 Penicillin
9 Motor racing should be banned.
10 Should motor racing be banned?
11 Women and equality
12 Should we be kind to people?
13 Should the government introduce compulsory education?
14 Private cars should be banned as they use too much fuel.
15 What can be done to stop people being cruel to each other?
16 Pollution is unavoidable.
17 Development must stop immediately.
18 The country should only be run by women.
19 Is crime bad?

EXERCISE 6.26

The paragraphs below are the introductions to essays. What is wrong with them? Discuss with your tutor what is wrong, and then write them out correctly.

1 Should we continue running the nation's airline? There is overwhelming evidence that we should keep the airline going. A large number of people are firmly convinced that we should not, as the money would be better spent on health services. In the newspapers last week there were several reports on the cost of maintaining the airline.

2 Computers are very necessary in secondary schools. Prof. Jones has argued that they are a waste of time in schools because the children will just play games on them all the time. Last week the government made a decision to buy computers for all the secondary schools in the country. Do the schools really need computers?

3 Last year the government decided to give up malaria control. The reason they gave was that it was too expensive. Is it right to give up a health programme on the grounds of expense? The government's argument was that the money could be better spent on other things. But it is definitely wrong to cut health programmes because people have a right to health care.

4 Last week Prof. Jones gave a lecture on the economic situation in Chad, suggesting that all the nations of the world should give money to help this country. Should we give aid to Chad? Certainly, money is useful because it allows Chad to decide itself how it will spend the money. However, there are many reasons why the world should not give aid in the form of money.

5 A few years ago it was suggested that English should be abandoned in schools because it was too time-consuming, and irrelevant to the needs of the country. Is this really true? There are a large number of people who would agree with this suggestion because they were never able to learn English well enough to get on.

| **EXERCISE 6.27** |

Essay Topics

Now write out a completed first paragraph, in full, for ten of the topics on page 139. You have done the first five already; do another five in the same way, and check that you are following the guidelines set out below.

A checklist for the introductory paragraph

In each of your introductory paragraphs have you included all of these?

1 Links between the topic and a recent event.
2 An **issue**, phrased as a **question**.
3 A section containing **one counter-argument** to your own point of view.
4 A **main idea statement**, which is your own point of view.

REMEMBER:
(a) An issue is a *question*. It does *not* contain supporting reasons.
(b) a main idea statement is a *statement*.
  • It is the *last sentence* of the paragraph.
  • It does *not* contain any supporting reasons.
  • It is the *answer* to the question posed by the issue.
  • Most of the words in the MIS are the *same* as those in the issue.

The Supporting Arguments

Now you have the introduction more or less sorted out, let us look at the **supporting arguments** in the argumentative essay.

Remember, you haven't written any of your own supports in the essay yet—only *one* of the opposition's.

The next stage in your planning of the essay is to make sure that your supporting arguments actually support your MIS. That sounds pretty simple, but in fact it often isn't.

| **EXERCISE 6.28** |

Look back at what you last wrote in the exercise. You were asked to write introductory paragraphs for ten of the topics on page 139 of this section of the unit. Take the MIS from *any five* of the ten paragraphs, and write three supports only for each one in this manner.

e.g. TOPIC _____
         ISSUE _____
         MIS _____
         SUPPORTS
         1 _____
         2 _____
         3 _____

Check what your neighbour has written. Do you think your neighbour's supports actually support the MIS?

Putting your supports into the essay

Each of your supports should be a paragraph of its own. So if you have three supports, your essay should have the following paragraphs:

Introduction

Support 1

Support 2

Support 3

Conclusion

Do not put more than one support into a paragraph. **Each support paragraph should begin with your support statement.** Begin your first support paragraph like this:

'The first reason why _____ is _____
   (put MIS here)   (put support here)

Your second will begin:

'The second reason why _____ is _____
   (put MIS here)   (your second support)

and so on.

Notice that *each* paragraph begins with a restatement of your MIS, and then clearly lays out what the support statement for that paragraph is going to be. This helps you to keep to the point, and helps the reader to remember what your main point is.

The rest of your paragraph explains your support statement, bringing in such things as quotations from sources, or references to other authorities in the field to give weight to your point of view.

Each support paragraph should conclude with an **example** that proves your support is a valid one. The examples should be as precise as possible, and they must *not* be made-up ones! **The more precise your examples, the more convincing your argument will be!** A precise example is an example that gives **names or numbers**.

Look at this support paragraph:

The first reason why the Nation should keep its airline is because it is an important item of international prestige. Whenever one of the aircraft is seen abroad, it indicates that the nation is wealthy enough, and commands expertise enough, to keep such an enormous item of investment running. As Jan Winters, the chairman of EuropAir said 'no one cares a jot whether the plane they see is paid for or not. All they look for is the logo on the tail.' (1983:45). Nations without an airline of their own are considered by international travellers as very undeveloped: not worth visiting. **It is for this reason that small nations like Singapore or Fiji have airlines of their own.**

Notice how the explanation deals only with the support covered by the first sentence, and the example makes the support valid.

EXERCISE 6.29

In the following exercise, each sentence is the beginning of the four support paragraphs for an essay entitled 'Should the death penalty be introduced?'

The MIS for this essay was: 'The death penalty should be introduced.'

Each one of the following openings is wrong in some way. Write them out, and then write down what you consider to be the correct openings.

1 The first reason is crime would be cut down if it was.

2 The second reason why is because of cost.

3 Finally we should introduce because an eye for an eye and a tooth for a tooth.

4 We need it because crime will be less.

You have corrected the sentences? Good. Now look at them, and decide if they

(a) are all supporting the MIS (or do they support a different one?);

(b) are in fact all different supports (or are some of them saying the same thing?).

EXERCISE 6.30

Look again at the supports you wrote in Exercise 6.28. Give *examples* to support your support statements for each of the five topics.

Discuss these with your partner. Which of you has the best examples?

EXERCISE 6.31

Essay Topics

Look at the support statements you have written for the topics in Exercise 6.28. Write out three supporting paragraphs for each of those five topics. Remember to include an *example* in each paragraph.

A checklist for writing support paragraphs

Do your support paragraphs contain all these elements?

1 Begin with a restatement of the MIS.

2 End with an example.

REMEMBER: Support paragraphs should *not* contain any suggestions!

The Concluding Paragraph

What do you put in the conclusion? Well, the one thing you should *not* put in is a summary of all your supports. That makes the essay repetitive and very boring to read.

What should go in is a **solution to the problem that was introduced by your issue**. In other words, your issue has shown that there is a problem with two sides to it. The two sentences that followed your issue showed these two sides. Your conclusion should try to show how the two sides could be reconciled.

For instance, if your issue has been 'Should the police be armed?', and your MIS was 'The police should not be armed', then the two sides of the issue must have been:

The police should be armed.
The police should not be armed.

Your conclusion could therefore be something like this:

Although it is clear that the police should definitely not be armed, there are occasions sometimes when it is necessary for the police to have weapons: when dealing with a dangerous criminal, for instance. The answer to this is perhaps to allow the police to carry weapons only when permitted to by a Judge or someone similar.

Notice that the only place you should put **suggestions** in an argumentative essay is at the end, in the conclusion.
    Suggestions are not supports!

EXERCISE 6.32

Look at the introductory paragraphs for *three* of the five topics you chose to write about in Exercise 6.31. For each of the three topics write the two alternative MISS you could have chosen from the issues. Then write a **suggestion** that would reconcile the two points of view.
e.g. MIS A _____
    MIS B _____
    Compromise suggestion _____

_____
Discuss these with your partner.

_____

EXERCISE 6.33

Essay Topics

Now you can try to write out the conclusions to the five essays you were writing in Exercise 6.31. Remember to write a sentence suggesting a compromise between the two sides you have shown in your introduction.

_____

So that is it. If you look at your completed work, you'll find that you have written a whole series of logically argued essays, which you have completed paragraph by paragraph.
    Well done!

The Preparation Sheet

In future each time you begin to plan an essay, you should lay out a **preparation sheet**, which will serve as your essay plan. Your preparation sheet should look something like this:

TOPIC:
ISSUE:
COUNTER-ARGUMENT:
MIS:
SUPPORTS: 1
               2
               3
               .

CONCLUDING SUGGESTION:

Every time you write an essay that asks you to defend your point of view, write a preparation sheet like this. It will help you argue your point **logically**.

An Overall Checklist

When you write your essay, remember the following things.
    The **Introduction** should have:
1 *links* between the topic and a recent event;
2 an *issue*, phrased as a question;
3 a section containing *one counter-argument* to your own point of view;
4 a *main idea statement*, which is your own point of view.
REMEMBER:
(a) An issue is a question; it does *not* contain supporting reasons.
(b) A MIS is a statement:
    • it is the *last sentence* of the paragraph;
    • it does *not* contain any supporting reasons;
    • it is the *answer* to the question posed by the issue;
    • most of the words in the MIS are the *same* as those in the issue.

    Each **support paragraph** should
1 begin with a restatement of the MIS;
2 contain only *one* support;
3 end with an *example*.
REMEMBER: Support paragraphs should *not* contain any suggestions.

    The **conclusion** should have a *solution* to the problem posed by your issue (a suggestion).
REMEMBER: This should *not* simply repeat your supports so far.

UNIT 7

Quoting Skills

PART 1

Referring to Books and Journals

There is a strict academic tradition about acknowledging sources of ideas and facts which you use in your own writing.

In academic life ideas are considered to be the 'property' of the person who first produced them. This is also true of facts: whoever compiles, say, a table of facts, is considered to be the 'owner' of this table. Anyone who uses the ideas or facts like the table, is expected to mention the name of the 'owner'—the person who first produced them.

If you copy other people's words without acknowledging those people it is like 'stealing' their ideas. At university you are expected to play the academic game according to the rules. If you copy another person's ideas and pretend that they are your own work, this is called 'plagiarism', and it is one of the most serious 'crimes' that an academic can commit.

Very few people could speak to an audience with ideas which are all their own creation. All of us use other people's ideas to build on, challenge or disagree with. Almost every book you read makes use of other people's ideas, and the author (if he's honest) is always careful to make clear which ideas he has borrowed, and from whom.

When you write academic essays you are expected to do the same. References to information and to ideas from other people (especially if they are authorities on the subject) add weight to your argument.

When you quote someone else's ideas or words, there are very strict conventions about how to do this, and you will be expected to follow these in all the work you do.

In Unit 3: Library Skills, you looked at the way **books and journals** are identified. This is not only important for you if you want to find a book in the library: it is also important for you when you want to:

(a) **quote** from the books you read; and

(b) set out a **bibliography** at the end of an essay or paper.

As you are expected to quote and provide a bibliography in every academic essay or paper you write, it is very important that you are able to find the necessary information that identifies a book or journal. You cannot quote the source of a fact or idea correctly unless you understand how to do this.

Look again at the Introduction section of Unit 3: Library Skills, before going on with the rest of this unit.

EXERCISE 7.1

Look at the front pages from the book below and on p. 154, and answer the following questions.

THE POLITICS OF LANGUAGE
1791-1819

OLIVIA SMITH

CLARENDON PRESS · OXFORD
1984

Oxford University Press, Walton Street, Oxford OX2 6DP

London New York Toronto
Delhi Bombay Calcutta Madras Karachi
Kuala Lumpur Singapore Hong Kong Tokyo
Nairobi Dar es Salaam Cape Town
Melbourne Auckland

and associated companies in
Beirut Berlin Ibadan Mexico City Nicosia

Oxford is a trade mark of Oxford University Press

Published in the United States
by Oxford University Press, New York

© Olivia Smith 1984

British Library Cataloguing in Publication Data
Smith, Olivia
The politics of language, 1791–1819.
1. Sociolinguistics   2. Great Britain —
Politics and government — 1760–1820
I. Title
320'.014   JN210

ISBN 0-19-812817-7

Typeset by Grestun Graphics, Abingdon, Oxon
Printed in Great Britain
at the University Press, Oxford
by David Stanford
Printer to the University

1 What is the title?

2 What is the author's name? (Get it **exactly** right!)

3 Who is the publisher?

4 When was this book published?

5 Is this the first edition of the book?

6 If it isn't the first edition, how many editions of the book has there been?

7 Where was it published?

EXERCISE 7.2

Look at the front page of the journal below, and answer the following questions:

S/1994 / R 888

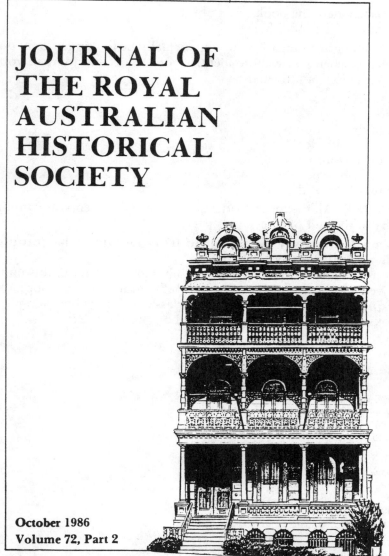

JOURNAL OF THE ROYAL AUSTRALIAN HISTORICAL SOCIETY

October 1986
Volume 72, Part 2

Registered by Australia Post. Publication No. NBH 0453, Category B.

1 What is the title of the journal?
2 What is the date of publication of the journal?
3 What is the number of the journal? (Two things are needed here!)
   Check the answers to Exercises 7.1 and 7.1 at the end of this Part to see if you are right!

REMEMBER: In the Library Skills unit, you were told that, to identify any book, you need to have *five* pieces of information:

These are:

1 Author.
2 Date of the actual edition you are using.
3 Title.
4 The place where the book was published.
5 The name of the publisher.

When you use a journal, you will normally be looking at only one particular article: so when you want to identify your source in a journal, you will need to have *six* pieces of information.

These are:

1 Author.
2 Date of publication.
3 Title of the article.
4 Title of the journal.
5 Volume and issue number of the journal.
6 Page numbers of the article.

REMEMBER: All of this is particularly necessary when you compile a **bibliography** at the end of an essay or paper.

No academic essay or paper can truly be said to be complete unless there is a bibliography at the end.

You will see how to put together a bibliography later in this unit.

However, before you put together a bibliography you must first know how to **put quotations correctly into your essays**, for the bibliography is a list of the books you have quoted from in the body of your text.

ANSWERS

EXERCISE 7.1—Book

1 *The Politics of Language.*
2 Olivia Smith.
3 Clarendon Press.
4 1984.
5 Yes.
6 First edition.
7 Oxford.

EXERCISE 7.2—Journal

1 *Journal of the Royal Australian Historical Society.*
2 1986.
3 2(2).

PART 2

Putting Quotations into an Essay

Using Your Sources

This section of the unit will cover the following:

1 **Putting a quotation into your essay.**
2 **Deciding how to quote.**

Putting a quotation into your essay

There are two kinds of quotation you can use:

(a) a **direct quotation**, where you use the writer's actual words; and
(b) an **indirect quotation**, where you summarize the writer's ideas and put them into your own words.

You must quote **whenever you are making use of another person's ideas**.

There is nothing wrong with using other people's ideas: that is, after all, what you are expected to do in an academic essay. However, you must *always* tell the reader when you are doing so.

When you put any quote in your essay, you must indicate **the source of your quote**. There are strict rules about how to do this properly.

A If you do not mention the author by name in your quote, you put the following in brackets ( ) at the end of the quote:

1 the **author's surname only**, followed by a comma;
2 the **date of publication** of the book, followed by a colon (:);
3 the **page number** of the reference.

e.g. 'Infectious disease is no longer the major cause of human deaths in Australia' (Morgan, 1967:261).

YOU MUST NOT CHANGE THE ORDER OF THESE THREE ITEMS.

B Sometimes you will actually want to mention the author of your quote in the text. If you do this, then immediately after the author's name you must put **in brackets** ( ):

1 the date of publication,
2 the page number.

e.g. Postgate (1975:245) believes that flush toilets are actually quite unhygenic.

or As Postage (1975:245) says, 'Flush toilets are actually quite unhygenic
devices'.

You do *not* put the author's name in again.

Perhaps the best way of learning how to use quotes properly is to look at
how a professional writer uses *both* these types of quotations in a text.

What follows is part of a well-written article from a journal of international
standing. The writer's argument is supported by facts which he has gathered
from other books and journals. These **source materials** are acknowledged in
the text and fully documented at the end.

Read through the extract and note where information from other books and
journals has been mentioned.

REMEMBER: Both direct and indirect quotations will be followed by a reference to the source in brackets.

Women Work Twice as Hard as Men*

Developing world

*(Peter Adamson reports on the results of recent research on woman's role in
world development)*

For millions of women in Africa, Asia and Latin America the working day commonly begins at 4.30 or 5.00 a.m. and ends sixteen hours later, as they struggle to meet the most basic needs of their families—for food, water, firewood, clothes, health care and a home.

The reason for this 'hundred-hour week' is that most women do two jobs—in the home and in agriculture.

According to the UN Food and Agriculture Organization in Rome (1980:29), women are responsible for at least 50 per cent of all food production. A study by the Economic Commission for Africa, for example (1977:123), has shown that women do 60 per cent to 80 per cent of all the agricultural work on the continent, plus 50 per cent of all animal 'husbandry' and 100 per cent of the food processing.

In one region studied—Bukaba in Tanzania—the men work an average of 1800 hours a year in agriculture and then their work is largely done. The women, on the other hand, work an average of 2600 hours a year in the field . . . and their work has only just begun. In the local Haya language the word 'to marry' literally means 'the man gets a hoe'.

It is the same story in India where women also do more than half of the subcontinent's agricultural work. 'It's usually thought that it is the man who is responsible for farm work, assisted by the women', writes Shanti Chakravorty (1976:57) in a study of India's wheat-growing Haryana State, 'but in most cases now it is the woman who does the farm work, assisted by the man'.

Taking labour in both home and field into account, the Haryana study found that the average working day for women was between 15 and 16 hours long. In one particular family, the work load of the three adult women and one twelve-year-old girl totalled 58 hours a day—12 hours doing household chores, 9 hours tending cattle, and 37 hours in agriculture. In a second family, a woman of seventy-five was putting in a ten-hour day.

In the case of younger women, such work loads are commonly combined with frequent pregnancy, childbirth and breast-feeding—exhausting processes for any woman's body, but particularly debilitating when compounded by inadequate food and long hours of back-breaking work in the fields (Chakravorty, 1976:57).

What all this adds up to is that one of the most important and most ignored health problems in the world of the 1980s is that millions of women are suffering from chronic exhaustion.

Unfortunately, numerous studies over the last five years indicate that the development effort itself can actually make matters worse (Rogers, 1980; Newland, 1979).

In the effort to improve nutrition, the prevalent myth that farmers are always men has meant that most of the agricultural training and technology has been geared to men's work. Tractors, for example, can shorten the work of the men who do the ploughing and lengthen the hours of the women who do the weeding.

In a now-famous African study, Esther Boserup (1970:43) noted that, in villages where modern technology had been introduced, the women's share of agricultural labour had risen from 55 per cent to 68 per cent.

If the effort to improve food production illogically bypasses women, then so does the effort to improve health. According to the World Health Organization (1978:16), about three-quarters of all illnesses in the developing world could be prevented by better nutrition, water and sanitation, immunization and health education, all areas in which women take major responsibility. But three-quarters of health budgets are being spent—by men on men—to provide expensive curative services to a small fraction of the population.

Similarly, the drive for literacy and education, which has seen school enrolment rates more than double in the developing countries since 1960, has also seen women come off second best. Two out of every three illiterate people in the world today are females. Yet as food producers and processors, as homemakers and health workers, and as the principal educators of the next generation, it is at least as important for women to be educated as men (WHO, 1978:16).

In the effort to improve nutrition, health and education—basic building blocks of a better life for the majority of the people—the rights, needs and contributions of women are being largely ignored. Recognizing the importance of women to the development effort is therefore not only a matter of principle to be enshrined in dusty declarations. It is an urgent practical issue. Nothing could do more to take the brakes off economic and social progress than the ending of discrimination against half the world's people.

Bibliography

Boserup, E., 1970, *Women's Role in Economic Development*, London, Allen & Unwin.

Chakravorty, Shanti, 1976, *Women's Contribution in India*, London, OUP.

E.C.A., 1977, *The New Economic Order—What Roles for Women?* Addis Abbaba, Economic Commission for Africa.

Newland, K., 1979, *The Sisterhood of Man*, New York, Worldwatch.

Rogers, B., 1980, *The Domestication of Women*, Chicago, Kogan Page Ltd.

U.N.D.P., 1980, 'Rural Women's Participation in Development', *Evaluation Study No. 3*, New York, U.N.D.P.

W.H.O., 1980, *Health, Population and Development*, Geneva, W.H.O.

*Adapted from P. Adamson and Eve Hall, 1980, 'Women Work Twice as Hard', *New Internationalist*, no. 89, p. 20.

You should have found only one direct quotation—from Shanti Chakravorty; you should have found *six* places in the text where indirect quotations are used. Did you find them all?

EXERCISE 7.3

For each quote write down:
(a) the **first six words** of text where each **indirect** quotation begins,
(b) the line these words occur on,
(c) the line where the indirect quotation ends,
(d) the source of the indirect quotation.

Set it out like this:

First six words	Begins line	Ends line	Source
1 _____	_____	_____	_____

REMEMBER: Do not include the *direct* quotes.

The facts Adamson refers to give authority to his argument. However, notice one important thing. **He has used very few DIRECT quotations: most of them are INDIRECT.** He has not merely taken the words of his originals but instead he has rewritten them so that, first, they fit in with his own style, and, second, **they relate more precisely to the exact point he is making.**

Make sure you do the same in the essays you write. Keep your direct quotation to a *minimum*.

If you put more than *two* direct quotations on each page of any essay, beware! You may not be making use of them properly.

REMEMBER: The aim of a course paper or an essay is to show your tutor that you have understood the topic and have done some reading. **Too many direct quotations** implies that you have not understood fully what you have read, and have merely copied the whole sentence blindly. **No reference to sources at all** implies that you have done no reading!

QUOTATIONS (both direct and indirect) MUST NOT BE USED AS A SUBSTITUTE FOR YOUR OWN THOUGHTS.

Direct or Indirect Quotations?

Many students have great difficulty incorporating quotations into their essays.

GOLDEN RULE—1

Whenever you put a quotation—direct or indirect—into a paragraph, the sentence in which it occurs must still remain grammatical.

Let us look at how you should incorporate quotations into your text.

Indirect quotations

EXERCISE 7.4

Look carefully at the indirect quotations again. Write down the phrases that Adamson uses to introduce the indirect quotations.

Introductory phrases

EXERCISE 7.5

There are, of course, many phrases that can be used to introduce information or ideas from other sources into your essay. Here are a few.

Smith points out . . .	Smith recognizes . . .
Smith reports . . .	According to Smith . . .
Smith notes . . .	To quote Smith: . . .
Smith observes . . .	As Smith has indicated . . .
Smith concludes . . .	Smith defines . . . as . . .

Which of these introductory phrases should be followed by 'that'? Write them out and include the word 'that' where it would be needed.

There are two things to pay special attention to here:

1 Notice once again that if the *original author's name* is included in the sentence, the name is not repeated in the source reference:

e.g. As Jones says (1980:56) 'Life is hard.'
but 'Life is hard' (Jones, 1980:56).

2 Notice how Adamson has put all his sources into his text: look at each sentence in which a quote occurs. Notice that each sentence reads as a *grammatically correct* one.

Direct quotations

The way a direct quotation is introduced into your text is important, because it must not interrupt the flow of your essay.

Look back at the Adamson article, and write down the phrase he used to connect the Chakravorty quote with his own text.

There are some special conventions which apply to direct quotations and you should follow them in your essays.

1 If for some reason you find it necessary to leave out part of a sentence because it is irrelevant and would make the quotation unnecessarily long, then three dots (. . .) are used to indicate this.

REMEMBER: The sentence must still be grammatical.

Example:

Original

'The most useful way of making a world survey is to identify families of languages, preferably using criteria such as those worked out by myself in 1933, showing relationships by origin and development' (Brook, 1978:98).

Quote

'The most useful way of making a world survey is to identify families of languages . . . showing relationships by origin and development' (Brook, 1978:98).

2 If you add something to a quotation to explain an abbreviation or a reference in the text, or for some other reason to make the quotation more intelligible, this addition should be enclosed in square brackets [ ].

Example:

'All the languages of the south-west coast [of New Britain] are Non-Austronesian, overlaid with a veneer of Austronesian' (Jones, 1981:71).

3 If a spelling mistake or other error has been made in the original text, you should copy the error. After the error, the word [*sic*] in square brackets is used to indicate that, even though the word seems unlikely, it is what actually appeared in the original.

Example:

'Life in the last century was much harder then [*sic*] life today' (Smith, 1983:45).

EXERCISE 7.6

The following sentences illustrate common mistakes in putting quotations into sentences. Rewrite each one correctly.

REMEMBER: Each one should read like a grammatically correct sentence.

1 According to Boserup, she says that women's share of agricultural work has increased rather than decreased where modern technology has been introduced.

2 Murray has defined health as 'Health is complete physical, mental and social well-being'.

3 Kivung reports that in 1981 our records show that 57 men were convicted of sexual offences against women.

4 As Pearson states that 'self motivation to learn is preferable to motivation imposed by external sources'.

5 Taking into account what Sir Holloway pointed out, is that, there are problems that are confronting education planners.

6 According to Goddard clearly stated that 'teachers must know when and how to intervene.'

7 In Holt, J's quote he stated that 'schools must be places where children feel at home'.

Deciding How to Quote

This section will give you some practice in deciding whether to use a direct or an indirect quotation.

There is of course no simple answer as to which sort of quotation you should use. Remember, however, that too many direct quotations in your essay can make it look as if you haven't thought for yourself.

EXERCISE 7.7

You have been given an assignment, 'Problems faced by women in the developing world in the 1980s', and you want to find quotes to illustrate a point you are making about the amount of work women do in the Third World.

Look back at the Adamson article and select one direct quote from the passage which would be suitable to include in the assignment.

Do not simply copy the Chakravorty quote—it is not appropriate anyway. *Look at what Adamson himself has to say*: it is not good practice to quote an author's reporting of other studies (you should quote them directly if at all possible).

To help you make a choice, here are some reasons why it might not be advisable to take the direct quotation from the first paragraph of the Adamson article.

(a) It could be easily paraphrased or shortened. Try rephrasing it in as few words as possible, and you will see how easy that could be:

(b) It is about Africa, Asia and Latin America, and therefore it is not directly relevant to the *topic* of the assignment.

You could make it relevant by putting in a phrase linking women in Melanesia to women in other parts of the world, at the beginning of the summary you have just written. Try it.

Do not forget to include the reference in brackets after your quotation.

Now look through the rest of the Adámson article and see if there is anything that is more relevant to your requirements. Write down your suggestion.

There is of course no right or wrong answer to this question. It is very much a matter of opinion. The quote that might perhaps be suitable is:

'One of the most important and most ignored health problems in the world of the 1980s is that millions of women are suffering from chronic exhaustion (Adamson:1980)'.

Compare this with your own suggestion, and decide which best meets the criteria.

Now practise putting the quotation about 'chronic exhaustion' from the first paragraph into a sentence, together with an acknowledgement of the source. Use any of the introductory phrases discussed earlier.

REMEMBER: Avoid 'that' with direct quotes.

Do not forget the source reference (in brackets) in your sentence, and that it should refer to Adamson.

Now do the same with the quotation that you have chosen. Write an introductory phrase and acknowledge the source at the end.

Indirect quotations

Using indirect quotations is much more difficult than using direct quotations, because you have to use your own words **to summarize what the author originally said**. It is more difficult to use indirect quotations than direct ones, but more useful because you can tailor your information to fit your requirements exactly.

In this part of the unit you will be getting more practice in using tables and graphs: look again at the section in Unit 6, Part 2, if you are not absolutely sure how to do this correctly.

EXERCISE 7.8

a Look at 'Women—The Facts' (pp. 168–9), and then answer these questions. Remember that your essay topic is 'Problems faced by women in the developing world in the 1980s'.

To make the point clear, it is always better to quote **examples** (remember the support paragraphs in Unit 6: Writing an Argumentative Essay). In this exercise compare two parts of the world: Africa and Europe.

1 According to the figures supplied by the Population Reference Bureau, what percentage of women marry below the age of twenty in Africa? What percentage do in Europe?

2 On average, how many more babies do women have in Africa than in Europe? (Fertility rate means number of babies per woman.)

3 What is the life expectancy for women in Europe and in Africa?

4 How much longer can women in Europe expect to live than women in Africa?

5 What percentage of women in Africa is engaged in agriculture as opposed to the European counterparts?

You will have noticed that the questions above are all to do with women's social life, and as such form the basis for one complete paragraph.

Join the information about women in Africa and in Europe into as few sentences as you can, and include a reference to the source of your information. No date is given in the source quotation, so you should leave it blank.

DO NOT MAKE UP INFORMATION THAT YOU DO NOT HAVE!

REMEMBER: Your reference is a quotation concerned with *women in Africa and in Europe*, and so it should not include information on where the women come from or what their husbands do. If you included this, it **would not be relevant**. You should only include information on *women* themselves.

Compare your answer with the suggestion at the end of this section.

b Now look again at the article, 'Women—The Facts'. You are looking for a reference to help you illustrate a point related to *women and education*. Bearing this in mind, answer the following questions:

1 What percentage of women in the Third World attend primary school as compared to the percentage of men?

2 What percentage of women in the Third World attend secondary school as compared to the percentage of men? What proportion of men to women is this?

3 What percentage of men are literate in the Third World? What percentage of women are literate?

Join all this information together into one short *indirect quote*, and acknowledge your source.

POSSIBLE ANSWERS

EXERCISE 7.8

Here are some possible indirect quotations to compare with your own attempts.

a According to the Population Reference Bureau, women in Africa marry much younger than their European counterparts: 7 per cent of European women are married before 20, while 44 per cent of African women are married by that age. African women have more babies: three times as many as women in Europe. They cannot expect to live as long as European women either, for their average life expectancy is 50, while a European woman can expect to live 25 years longer.

b According to figures given by the Population Reference Bureau, 53 per cent of women attend primary school in the developing world, as opposed to 70 per cent of men. When they reach secondary school age, only 28 per cent of women go on, while 42 per cent of men continue, which is twice as many. The resulting literacy rates reflect this trend: 52 per cent of males are literate in the third world, while only 32 per cent of women are.

c A study by the Population Reference Bureau has shown that, on average, women in the developing world can expect to live to the age of 76, and will have two children. Nearly all (98 per cent) are literate, and 84 per cent of them attend school until the age of seventeen. Perhaps because of this it should be no surprise that very few (8 per cent) marry before the age of twenty.

It would be possible to write something about the varying roles of men and women relying only on the figures in the columns for the whole of the *developing world* and the whole of the *developed world*.

Try the same technique to produce a reference summarizing the information in these two columns, referring particularly to social and educational matters. Remember to **acknowledge your source**.

These three references to the statistical chart each give a different focus, which would be relevant to different points being made in an essay. Rephrasing information into a clear, concise form which is directly related to a particular topic is the key to good essay writing.

EXERCISE 7.9

Assignment

Look at the following article, 'Industrialised World', from *New Internationalist*, no. 89, 1980, p. 21, and the chart, 'Women's work—the facts', from *New Internationalist*, no. 90, 1980, pp. 10–11.

Write a short essay (about 500 words) on 'The Differences between the Roles of Women in the Developed and the Developing World'.

You may use these two references, or you may use any other materials you think relevant, provided you acknowledge your sources properly.

Industrialised World

Eve Hall looks at ten years of women's liberation in the developed world and finds that everywhere women still work longer for less.

One of the greatest economic and social changes of the post-war years has gone largely unnoticed. It is that more and more women are going out to work. Today in the United States, in Japan and in the United Kingdom, almost 40 per cent of the work force is female.

In theory this should mean that women are becoming better-off, liberated, equal. But in practice it is a different story.

Most women now work far longer hours than men—in factory, shop or office as well as in the home as cook, cleaner, child rearer, shopper and homemaker. This 'double burden' means that the average woman who goes out to work is now putting in an 80-hour working week—twice as long as most men.

So equality depends not only on women sharing in paid employment but also on men sharing in the tasks of the home. At the moment husbands in all industrialised countries contribute very little to domestic work and recent research shows that this contribution does not increase when the wife goes out to work. American researcher Joan Vanek,

for example, found that the average father in the United States spends only 12 minutes a day with his children. Overall, women's unpaid work in the U.S.A. is estimated at about 40 per cent of the Gross Domestic Product.

But even in the work-place itself, women's wages are everywhere lower than men's. In the U.K., women are paid an average of 25 per cent less. In the U.S.A., they are paid 40 per cent less. And this is despite equal pay legislation in most industrialised countries.

The reasons why women earn less than men go deeper than legislation. And again the main cause is the 'double burden' of home responsibilities which means that many women have to take part-time jobs, or less demanding jobs, and that they have less time for training and less opportunity for promotion.

As children, girls are educated and conditioned either for no employment at all or for more menial and lower-paid jobs. As workers, they are crowded into industries like textiles, food, clothing, retailing—where they compete with each other for low-paid and insecure jobs which require little skill or training and offer little chance of promotion. A recent survey in Sweden shows that women have a choice of about 25 different occupations whereas a man chooses from over 300 careers. Indeed certain countries, says the OECD, 'have come to rely on a supply of female labour which costs little and enjoys little protection'.

The result of this inequality is that women have more than their fair share of poverty. And particularly hard-hit are the families dependent on a woman's earnings.

Single parent families are increasing in almost every industrialised country. In Britain at least 600,000 families are now headed by single mothers and the number is growing by 6 per cent a year. The main cause is the rise in divorce rates which have doubled in many countries (including both the U.S.A. and the U.S.S.R.) during the last 15 years.

It is these single-parent families, says the International Labour Organisation, which make up the fastest rising group in any classification of the poor population. Even after the receipt of benefits, the incidence of poverty is only just below that of pensioners and is much higher than in any other group.

As the ILO notes, pensioners are the poorest social group in the industrialised world. But here too it is the women who are worst off—partly because they tend to live longer than men and partly because inequality during their working lives is reflected in reduced pensions. In the United States, for example, the 8 million women who are over the age of 65 make up by far the poorest group of people in America—with almost half of them living below the official poverty line.

For women at work, the final irony is that the trades unions—which have done so much to improve the pay, conditions and benefits of work forces in the industrialised world—are also dominated by men. In America's garment industry, 80 per cent of the union members are women but 21 of the 22 member board of the union are men. In New Zealand only 15 of the country's 323 unions have any women executives despite the fact that women carry over a third of all union membership cards.

The first half of the U.N. Decade for Women (1975–80) has now gone and the vast majority of women in the industrialised countries have seen little or no benefit. Equal-pay legislation in almost all industrialised countries has been one of the big achievements of these five years. The task for the next five years is to achieve equal work which will give substance to equal pay. The biggest barrier is that working women now do two jobs. And overcoming that barrier is as much of a challenge to men as it is to women.

If women are to be fully integrated into active economic, social and political participation in planning and decision making of their societies it is imperative that their presence in demographic and other statistics is "unveiled" to provide a more valid base for programmes concerned with improving women's lot in the world ... To say that "women don't count" is often the literal truth, thus giving substance to the cliche that they are 'the forgotten 50 per cent' of the world's population.

—Gustavo Perez-Ramirez, Deputy Director, UN Population Division.

The trouble is that even accurate statistics and methodologically sound research most often fall on deaf ears. In this respect, statistics relating to women are similar to those of casualties of war. There seems to be an inability, particularly amongst politicians, diplomats and academics, to see the relevance or point of such information or even in a sense to hear it.

—Elizabeth Reid, Principal Officer, World Conference to UN Decade for Women.

Women
The Facts

Young and Old
The percentage of women under the age of fifteen in poor countries is abou twice as high as in rich countries. But the percentage of women over the age of fifty is only about half as high.

Babies
On average, women in poor countries tend to have twice as many babies as women in rich countries. About four out of ten under-twenty year-olds are married in the developing world. In the industrialised world the proportio is only about one in ten.

Life Expectancy
A woman's life expectancy in Africa i about fifty years as opposed to sevent five years in Europe. One reason is tha the chances of dying in the first year can be up to ten times higher in devel oping countries.

Agriculture
In the developing world, seven out of every ten women are employed in agriculture.

Schooling
In the developing world, about seven out of ten boys and five out of ten gir are enrolled in primary schools.

Apartheid by Sex

Women are half the world's people ...

Do two-thirds of the world's working hours ...

Receive one tenth of the world's income ...

And own only one hundredth of the world's property ...

Family Planning

WE WANT MORE CHILDREN	WE DO NOT WANT ANY MORE CHILDREN
	USING CONTRACEPTION
	NOT USING CONTRACEPTION

In most developing countries, more than half the married women aged 14 to 19 don't want any more children. But of those, only about half are using any modern contraceptive method.

Education

Two out of every three illiterate people in the world are women.

Food

Almost all the training and technology for improving agriculture is given to men ...

50 per cent of the agricultural production and all of the food processing is the responsibility of the women.

Health

80 per cent of health budgets are used to cure the illnesses of a minority through the training and equipping of doctors who are usually men ...

80 per cent of all illness in the Third World could be prevented by better nutrition, water supply, sanitation, immunisation and preventive health education—the responsibility for which is usually taken by women.

	World	Developed World	Developing World	Africa	Asia	Latin America	Europe	North America
Total Female Population (in millions)	2,201	584	1617	237	1256	180	248	126
Aged 0 to 14 years	34	22	39	44	38	40	21	22
Aged over 50 years	17	29	13	11	13	13	31	28
Total Fertility Rate	3.8	2.0	4.4	6.4	3.9	4.5	2.0	1.8
Married before age 20	30	8	39	44	42	16	7	11
Life Expectancy (male/female)	56/59	68/76	54/56	47/50	57/59	61/66	69/75	69/77
Infant Mortality Rate (male/female)	103/92	24/18	116/104	151/129	108/99	90/80	25/19	16/12
Women Employed in Agriculture	49	13	70	73	69	12	20	1
in School aged 6 to 11 (male/female)	76/64	94/94	70/53	59/43	73/54	78/78	95/96	99/99
in School aged 12 to 17 (male/female)	55/46	84/85	42/28	39/24	43/28	58/54	81/80	95/95
of Adults Literate (male/female)	67/54	98/97	52/32	33/15	56/43	76/70	96/93	99/99

res extracted from the 'World's Women Data Sheet' published by the Population Reference Bureau in collaboration with UNICEF.
ies of the complete Data Sheet may be obtained by writing to the PRB at 1337 Connecticut Avenue N.W. Washington D.C. 20036, USA
e $ 1.00 or equivalent).

Population

Research and advice on family planning is usually directed towards women . . .

Decisions on family size are usually taken by men.

Women's work - the facts

Over the last 30 years women have joined the paid work force in ever increasing numbers. And despite claims to the contrary most women work because they have to — to provide for their families. Still, almost everywhere women are paid less than men for equal work. In addition work in the household continues and women must shoulder most of this burden. The New Internationalist illustrates some of the facts behind women's work.

More women working

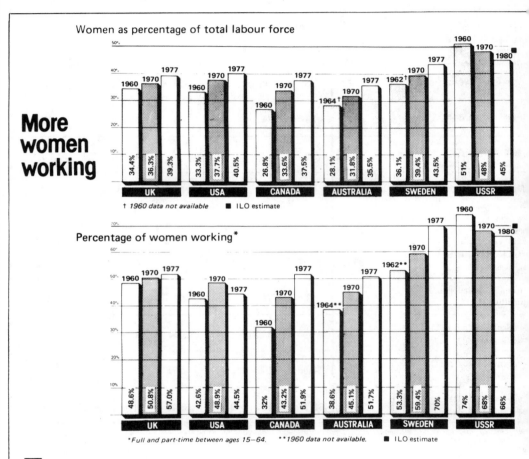

Women as percentage of total labour force

	UK	USA	CANADA	AUSTRALIA	SWEDEN	USSR
	34.4% 36.3% 39.3%	33.3% 37.7% 40.5%	26.8% 33.6% 37.5%	28.1% 31.8% 35.5%	36.1% 39.4% 43.5%	51% 48% 45%

† 1960 data not available   ■ ILO estimate

Percentage of women working*

	UK	USA	CANADA	AUSTRALIA	SWEDEN	USSR
	48.6% 50.8% 57.0%	42.6% 48.9% 44.5%	32% 43.2% 51.9%	38.6% 45.1% 51.7%	53.3% 59.4% 70%	74% 68% 66%

*Full and part-time between ages 15—64.   **1960 data not available.   ■ ILO estimate

THERE HAS been an explosion of women into the labour force since the early 60s in nearly all developed countries. While only four out of ten American women worked outside the home in 1960, by 1977 nearly six out of ten did. In Sweden 70 per cent of all women are salaried workers. As a result the overall picture is slowly changing. Women now comprise around 40 per cent of the total labour force in most Western nations. As women assume a more central place in the workforce traditional barriers to equal pay and a wider choice of jobs will face increasing challenge.

For the Third World statistics are less reliable and less complete. However, according to International Labour Office figures the picture is strikingly different. The percentage of women in the 'formal' job market has actually decreased since 1950. The gradual shift from subsistence to cash economy appears to be at the expense of women. For example 32 per cent of African women were considered part of the labour force in in 1950, only 24 per cent will qualify in 1980.

Women need to work ...

For a variety of reasons — marital breakdown, death of husband or husband's migration to work — more and more women are now chief provider for themselves and their families.

In the **English-speaking Caribbean** one-third of all families are headed by women.

In **Venezuela** 25 per cent of all families depend on the earnings of women breadwinners.

In the **US** in 1977 only 16 per cent of all families were the traditional nuclear type. Nearly 15 per cent of all families are led by women.

In the **UK** at least 600,000 families are now headed by single mothers. And that figure is increasing by 6 per cent yearly.

but they still get less pay

On a **world wide average** women earn only 40—60 per cent of the income of men.

In the **US** women earn only 60 cents for every dollar earned by men.

In the **UK** women are paid an average of 25 per cent less than men.

In **Canada** in 1975 unequal pay for women was responsible for half the difference in earnings between all men and women working full-time.

In **South Korea** in 1977 80 per cent of all workers making less than $42 per month were women. More than half of them worked 8—10 hours a day and one-third more than 15 hours a day.

Women's work is not recognized

Women's unpaid work in the home or in the fields is usually ignored in labour statistics. As a result this work becomes 'invisible' and is not seen as 'real' work.

Rural women in Third World countries as a whole account for at least 50 per cent of all **food production**.

In Africa 60—80 per cent of all **agricultural work** is done by women.

In the Himalayan region 70 per cent of agricultural work is done by women.

Domestic labour — child-minding and keeping house are crucial to everyday life. The average Western housewife spends 3,000 — 4,000 unsalaried hours a year on housework. Despite modern conveniences, studies show the amount of housework has not decreased in the last 50 years.

Photo · Sally Greenhill

*Sources — ILO Yearbooks of Labour Statistics.·
OECD Labour Force Statistics.*

*UN State of the World's Women Report 1979
Housewife by Anne Oakley.*

PART 3

Writing a Bibliography

A bibliography is an alphabetical list of all the sources a person has used. It is set out at the end of each piece of written work. **It must be in alphabetical order**, and each entry *must* be laid out in a strictly ordered sequence.

EXERCISE 7.10

Look at the following bibliography and the way it is arranged.
(a) In what order are the books?
(b) What is written first in each entry?
(c) Where does the book title appear?
(d) How is the title of the book indicated?
(e) What usually comes last in each entry?
   Some of the entries in the bibliography are for journals, not for books.
   You should be able to recognize the difference immediately from the entry itself. Write down three features for a *journal* entry that you do not find in a *book* entry.

Note: Books and journals are not separated in a bibliography.

   The answers to these questions can be found at the end of this Part.

Bibliography

Curwen, E. C., and C. Hatt, 1953, <u>Plough and Pasture: The Early History of Farming</u>, New York, Abelard-Schuman.
Forde, C. D., 1931, 'Hopi Agriculture and Land Ownership', <u>Journal of the Royal Anthropological Institute</u>, 41:357-405.
Harner, M. J., 1970, 'Population Pressure and the Social Evolution of the Agriculturalist', <u>Southwestern Journal of Anthropology</u>, 26:68-86.
Hogbin, H. I., 1964, <u>A Guadalcanal Society: The Kaoka Speakers</u>, New York, Holt, Rinehart & Winston.
Jacobsen, T., 1943, 'Primitive Democracy in Ancient Mesopotamia', <u>Journal of Near Eastern Studies</u>, 11(3):1521-72.
Josephy, A. M., Jr., 1968, <u>The Indian Heritage of America</u>, New York, Alfred A. Knopf.

Pospisil, L. J., 1963, <u>The Kapauku Papuans of West New Guinea</u>, New York, Holt, Rinehart & Winston.

Sanders, W. T., and B. J. Price, 1968, <u>Mesoamerica: The Evolution of a Civilization</u>, New York, Random House.

Service, E. R., 1958, <u>Profiles in Ethnology</u>, New York, Harper & Row.

Uchendu, V. L., 1965, <u>The Igbo of Southeast Nigeria</u>, New York, Holt, Rinehart & Winston.

Ucko, P. J., and G. W. Dimbleby, 1969, <u>The Domestication and Exploitation of Plants and Animals</u>, Chicago, Aldine Publishing Company.

A bibliography gives all the information a reader needs to find the source in a library. The information for each entry should always be presented in the same strict order. This order is used because the libraries in the academic world catalogue their books by filing the information about them in this same sequence. This means that everyone can find quickly and easily the books they are searching for, provided the writer of the paper writes his bibliography correctly.

For a **book** the bibliographical entry should appear like this:

1 The author's surname, followed by his initials or first names, *exactly as they appear in the book.*
2 Date of publication.
3 Title of the book <u>underlined</u> (in printed books and journals the title is written in *italic type*).
4 Place of publication.
5 Name of the publisher.

e.g.

Carrol, V., 1975, <u>Pacific Atoll Populations</u>, Honolulu University Press, Hawaii.

Note: 1 The way the entry is punctuated.
      2 Where there are *two* authors, the second author's initials come **before** his surname, exactly as it appears in the book.

For an **article in a journal** the entry is:

1 The author's surname, followed by his initials or first names.
2 Date of publication.
3 Title of the article in 'inverted commas'.
Pay special attention to the difference from the entry for books.
4 Title of the journal <u>underlined</u> (or given in *italics*).

e.g.

Conroy, J., 1973, 'Urbanization in Papua New Guinea: A Development Constraint', <u>Economic Record</u>, 49(2):76-88.

After the title of the journal comes:

5 The volume number, and the issue within that volume (in brackets),

6 The page numbers of the article.

Where there are two authors to a book, do not be tempted to change their names around to fit in with the alphabetical ordering. The first author is usually the more important of the two, or the more well-known one, and so this name must stay first in your bibliographical entry: it is put in the appropriate alphabetical place in the list.

REMEMBER: The initials of the second author come **before** his name.

Important note: You only underline titles when they are the titles of **published** books or journals.

If you wish to refer to a title that belongs to an unpublished book, then put the title in **inverted commas** (' ') in the same way that you refer to journal articles.

You would do this for:

(a) **unpublished papers** (you indicate this by writing 'MS' after the title);

(b) **PhD theses** (you indicate this by writing 'PhD thesis' after the title).

> e.g. Brown, J., 1985, 'The Interface between School and College', PhD thesis, University of Hawaii.

EXERCISE 7.11

This bibliography has some mistakes in it. Rewrite it correctly.

```
Lipton, M., 'Urban Bias and Food Policy in Poor Countries'
   Food Policy, Vol I no 4, pp 41-52, 1975
E. E. Echholm, 1976, Losing Ground: Environmental Stress and
   World Food Prospects, New York, Norton.
Wortman, S., 1976, 'Food and Agriculture' Scientific American,
   September Vol, 30-9.
Schneider, S., and L. Mesirow, 1976, The Genesis Strategy,
   New York, Plenum.
Groth, E., 1975, 'Increasing the Harvest', Environment, No I,
   28-39.
```

Check answers to this exercise at the end of this unit, and then do Exercise 7.12.

EXERCISE 7.12

Look at the following title-pages of some books and journals, and write a bibliography using all of them.

MAKE SURE THAT YOU HAVE DONE THIS CORRECTLY BEFORE YOU BEGIN THE ASSIGNMENT ON PAGE 186.

FROM SUBSERVIENCE TO STRIKE

Industrial Relations in
the Banking Industry

JOHN HILL

Typeset by University of Queensland Press
Printed and bound by Hedges & Bell Pty Ltd, Melbourne

Distributed in the United Kingdom, Europe, the Middle East,
Africa, and the Caribbean by Prentice-Hall International,
International Book Distributors Ltd, 66 Wood Lane End, Hemel
Hempstead, Herts., England.

*National Library of Australia
Cataloguing-in-Publication data*

Hill, John, 1940–.
    From subservience to strike.

    Bibliography.
    Includes index.
    ISBN 0 7022 1830 8.
    ISBN 0 7022 1834 0 (pbk.).
    1. Australian Bank Employees Union – History.
    2. Trade-unions – Bank employees – Australia –
    History. I. Title.

331.88'113321'0994

Library of Congress Cataloging in Publication Data

Hill, John, 1940–
    From subservience to strike.

    Bibliography: p.
    Includes index.
    1. Australian Bank Employees' Union – History.
2. Trade-unions – Bank Employees – Australia – History.
3. Bank employees – Australia – History. I. Title.
HD6894.B262A925   331.88'113321'0994   82–2684
ISBN 0-7022-1830-8   AACR2
ISBN 0-7022-1834-0 (pbk.).

Studies in Economic and Social History

The Economic Effects of the Two World Wars on Britain

Second Edition

Alan S. Milward

First edition 1972
Second edition 1984

Published by
Higher and Further Education Division
MACMILLAN PUBLISHERS LTD
London and Basingstoke
Companies and representatives
throughout the world

Typeset by
Wessex Typesetters Ltd
Frome, Somerset

Printed in Hong Kong

British Library Cataloguing in Publication Data
Milward, Alan
    The economic effects of the two world wars on
    Britain.—2nd ed.—(Studies in economic and
    social history)
    1. Great Britain—Economic conditions—1918–1945
    I. Title   II. Series
    330.941′083   HC256.8
    ISBN 0–333–36954–8

Journal of International Studies

MILLENNIUM

Vol. 15 No. 1   Spring 1986

Millennium Publishing Group

London School of Economics

MILLENNIUM: Journal of International Studies

London School of Economics
Houghton Street
London, WC2A 2AE
Telephone: 01-405 7686
Ext. 2407/8

Vol. 15, No.1

Table of Contents

Abstracts

Articles

5/330/A938

AUSTRALIAN ECONOMIC PAPERS

VOL. 24   **DECEMBER, 1985**   **No. 45**

ANNUAL SUBSCRIPTION: $18   Published twice a year

Notional Syllabuses

*A taxonomy and its relevance to foreign language
curriculum development*

D. A. WILKINS

*Department of Linguistic Science
University of Reading*

OXFORD UNIVERSITY PRESS

Oxford University Press, Walton Street, Oxford OX2 6DP

OXFORD LONDON GLASGOW NEW YORK
TORONTO MELBOURNE WELLINGTON CAPE TOWN
IBADAN NAIROBI DAR ES SALAAM
DELHI BOMBAY CALCUTTA MADRAS KARACHI
KUALA LUMPUR SINGAPORE JAKARTA HONG KONG TOKYO

ISBN 0 19 437071 2

© Oxford University Press, 1976

First published 1976
Reprinted 1977, 1978

Printed in Great Britain by The Camelot Press Ltd. Southampton

ANSWERS

EXERCISE 7.10

(a) **Alphabetical order**. Books and periodicals (journals) are not kept separate.
(b) The author's **surname**.
(c) If it is a book title, it comes *after* the author's surname and initials. If it is a journal title, it comes *after* the title of the article.
(d) It is underlined.
(e) The **name of the publisher**, if it is a book; the **page numbers of the article**, if it is a journal.
   Journal entries differ from book entries:
1 There are two titles in the entry: the article title (in inverted commas), and the journal title (underlined).
2 The volume and issue numbers are included.
3 The publisher and the place of publication do *not* appear in a journal entry.

EXERCISE 7.11

REMEMBER: Alphabetical order.

Echholm, E. C., 1976, Losing Ground: Environmental Stress and World Food Prospects, New York, Norton.
Groth, E., 1975, 'Increasing the Harvest', Environment, I(1), 28-39.
Lipton, M., 1975, 'Urban Bias and Food Policy in Poor Countries', Food Policy, I(4), 41-52.
Schneider, S., and L. Mesirow, 1976, The Genesis Strategy, New York, Plenum.
Wortman, S., 1976, 'Food and Agriculture', Scientific American, September, 30-9.

Note: There are only two books here; the rest are journal articles.

EXERCISE 7.12

Bronfenbrenner, Martin, 1985, 'Japan Faces Affluence', Australian Economic Papers, 24(45), 227-41.
Hill, John, 1983, From Subservience to Strike: Industrial Relations in the Banking Industry, Queensland, University of Queensland Press.
Jentleson, Bruce W., 1986, 'The Political Basis for Trade in US-Soviet Relations', Journal of International Studies, 15(1), 27-47.
Milward, Alan S., 1984, The Economic Effect of the Two World Wars on Britain, 2nd edition, London, Macmillan.
Wilkins, D. A., 1976, Notional Syllabuses, England, Oxford University Press.

   Did you get all of this right?
   If you didn't, put it all away for a few days, and then try again.
DO NOT DO THE ASSIGNMENT UNTIL YOU ARE SURE YOU CAN DO THIS EXERCISE PROPERLY.

Some Additional Guidelines

Although there is neither time nor space here to practise all the aspects of quoting sources, you may find the following guidelines useful.

1 Sometimes you will find a book that is made up of short chapters written by different people. The person who has chosen the chapters and put them together into a book is called the editor, and you will find the book in the library catalogued under the editor's name.

Refer to an **edited book** like this:

Brown, J. L. (ed.), 1979, The Search for Peace, Sydney, World Press.

If you wish to refer only to *one chapter* in this book, you can write your entry like this:

Walker, M., 1979, 'The Post-War Years' in J. L. Brown (ed.), The Search for Peace, Sydney, World Press, pp. 45-83.

2 Refer to an **encyclopaedia** like this:

Colliers Encyclopaedia, 1968, 'Frog', vol. 10, London, Crowell-Collier Education Corporation, pp. 421-7.

3 Refer to a **course handout** like this:

Worsely, P., 1970, 'What Is Socialization?', 12.101 Course Handout, U.P.N.G.

4 For a **newspaper article** set out your reference like this:

Blair, W. B., 1968, 'Aboriginal Houses Inferior Houses', Herald (Melbourne), May 8, p. 10.

or

'Rabaul on Volcano Alert', 1983, Post-Courier (Port Moresby), Nov. 1, p. 3.

Use this second version where the author's name is not known.

EXERCISE 7.13

On the following pages you will find examples of the beginnings of books and journals. Put these together to form a bibliography.

In the case of journal articles, you must take your source to be the article indicated by an arrow (⟶).

REMEMBER:
(a) Put them in alphabetical order.
(b) Set out a journal article reference differently from one for a book.
(c) Quote the author's name correctly.

THE MONEY SUPPLY AND THE EXCHANGE RATE

Edited by W. A. Eltis and P. J. N. Sinclair

Oxford University Press, Walton Street, Oxford OX2 6DP

London Glasgow New York Toronto
Delhi Bombay Calcutta Madras Karachi
Kuala Lumpur Singapore Hong Kong Tokyo
Nairobi Dar es Salaam Cape Town
Melbourne Auckland
and associate companies in
Beirut Berlin Ibadan Mexico City

Published in the United States
by Oxford University Press, New York

© Oxford University Press 1981

British Library Cataloguing in Publication Data

The money supply and the exchange rate.
1. Money supply — Great Britain
2. Foreign exchange
I. Eltis, W. A.   II. Sinclair, P. J. N.
332.4'0941   HG939.5
ISBN 0-19-877168-1

Printed in Northern Ireland
at The Universities Press (Belfast) Ltd.

READINGS IN LABOUR ECONOMICS

Edited readings with commentaries by J.E.KING

Oxford University Press, Walton Street, Oxford OX2 6DP

OXFORD LONDON GLASGOW
NEW YORK TORONTO MELBOURNE WELLINGTON
KUALA LUMPUR SINGAPORE JAKARTA HONG KONG TOKYO
DELHI BOMBAY CALCUTTA MADRAS KARACHI
NAIROBI DAR ES SALAAM CAPE TOWN

Published in the United States by
Oxford University Press, New York

British Library Cataloguing in Publication Data

Readings in labour economics.
   1. Labor supply – Addresses, essays, lectures
   I. King, John Edward
   331.1'2'08   HD5706   79-41096

   ISBN 0-19-877132-0
   ISBN 0-19-877133-9 Pbk

Typesetting by Anne M. Joshua, Oxford
and Printed in Great Britain by
Richard Clay (The Chaucer Press) Ltd,
Bungay, Suffolk

THE JOURNAL OF THE POLYNESIAN SOCIETY

VOLUME 95 No. 4 DECEMBER 1986

THE POLYNESIAN SOCIETY

AUCKLAND   NEW ZEALAND

Volume 95   December 1986   Number 4

CONTENTS

ISSN 0030-7653

OXFORD ECONOMIC PAPERS

VOLUME 37   JUNE 1985   NUMBER 2

CONTENTS

CLARENDON PRESS · 1985

CONTENTS

continued on outside back cover

ISSN 0360–5442
ENEYDS 11(6) 545–642 (1986)

PERGAMON PRESS

New York · Oxford · Beijing · Frankfurt
Sào Paulo · Sydney · Tokyo · Toronto

Teaching English as a Second Language

J A Bright
G P McGregor

LONGMAN GROUP LTD
London

*Associated companies, branches and representatives
throughout the world*

© Longman Group Ltd 1970

First published 1970

New impression 1971

ISBN 0 582 54003 8

*Made and printed in Great Britain by
William Clowes & Sons Limited, London, Colchester and Beccles*

Tom McArthur

The Written Word

A course in controlled composition

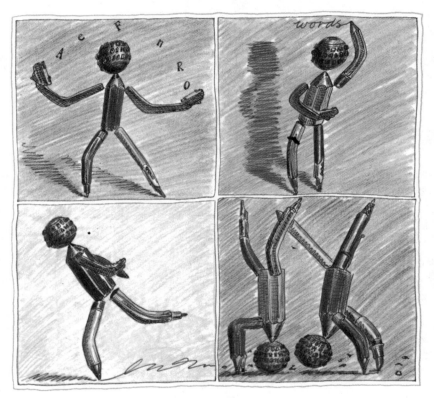

Book 2

Oxford

Oxford University Press
Walton Street, Oxford OX2 6DP

London New York Toronto
Delhi Bombay Calcutta Madras Karachi
Kuala Lumpur Singapore Hong Kong Tokyo
Nairobi Dar es Salaam Cape Town
Melbourne Auckland

and associated companies in
Beirut Berlin Ibadan Mexico City Nicosia

OXFORD is a trade mark of Oxford University Press.

ISBN 0 19 451361 0

The publishers would like to thank the following for
permission to reproduce photographs.

Anglo-Australian Observatory
Elliott Erwitt/John Hillelson Agency
Christopher Hume/Camera Press
Mark Mason
Axel Poignant
Rosie Potter
Jeremy Rowland

Cover illustration by Peter Till

Typeset by Tradespools Ltd, Frome, Somerset
Printed in Hong Kong

JANET RAMAGE

ENERGY
A GUIDEBOOK

Oxford University Press, Walton Street, Oxford OX2 6DP

London Glasgow New York Toronto
Delhi Bombay Calcutta Madras Karachi
Kuala Lumpur Singapore Hong Kong Tokyo
Nairobi Dar es Salaam Cape Town
Melbourne Auckland
and associated companies in
Beirut Berlin Ibadan Mexico City Nicosia

Oxford is a trade mark of Oxford University Press

First published 1983 as an Oxford University Press paperback
and simultaneously in a hardback edition

British Library Cataloguing in Publication Data
Ramage, Janet
Energy. — (OPUS)
1. Force and energy
I. Title II. Series
531'.6 QC73
ISBN 0–19–219169–1
ISBN 0–19–289157–X Pbk

Library of Congress Cataloging in Publication Data
Ramage, Janet, 1932–
Energy, a guidebook. (OPUS)
Bibliography: p. Includes index.
1. Power resources. 2. Power (Mechanics)
I. Title. II. Series.
TJ163.2.R345 1983 333.79 82–14207
ISBN 0–19–219169–1
ISBN 0–19–289157–X (pbk.)

Typeset by Wyvern Typesetting Ltd, Bristol
Printed in Great Britain by
Richard Clay (The Chaucer Press) Ltd
Bungay, Suffolk

ESSAYS IN
EUROPEAN
ECONOMIC
HISTORY

1500—1800

EDITED

for the Economic History Society

BY

PETER EARLE

CLARENDON PRESS
OXFORD
1974

Oxford University Press, Ely House, London W. 1

GLASGOW NEW YORK TORONTO MELBOURNE WELLINGTON
CAPE TOWN IBADAN NAIROBI DAR ES SALAAM LUSAKA ADDIS ABABA
DELHI BOMBAY CALCUTTA MADRAS KARACHI LAHORE DACCA
KUALA LUMPUR SINGAPORE HONG KONG TOKYO

CASEBOUND ISBN 0 19 877054 5

© OXFORD UNIVERSITY PRESS 1974

*Printed in Great Britain by
Richard Clay (The Chaucer Press), Ltd.,
Bungay, Suffolk*

ISSN 0022-5142
Volume 38, Number 3
1987

Journal of the Science of Food and Agriculture

Published for the
Society of
Chemical Industry
by
Elsevier Applied
Science Publishers

J. SCI. FOOD AGRIC. VOL. 38 NO. 3 1987

(Abstracted/indexed in: *BIOSIS (Biological Abstracts); Biological and Agricultural Index; Chemical Abstracts; Index Medicus; Current Contents; Science Citation Index*)

CONTENTS

PART 4

Understanding Footnotes

There is another system for acknowledging sources within a text which is common in textbooks. This is the use of **footnotes**.

You should become familiar with the system of footnoting, because you will come across it in your reading. However, **you should not use footnotes in your essays unless specifically instructed to do so by one of your tutors**.

Footnotes are marked in the text by a small number at the place where the writer wants to clarify a point he has made, or to mention something that he does not want to put in the main body of the text. These small numbers allow the writer to list his notes consecutively as they appear in the text.

The notes themselves can be placed in one of two places:

1 At the foot of the same page as the small number, under a ruled line, or in different print.
2 At the end of the text, before the bibliography. Sometimes the footnotes at the end appear under the title 'References'.

Footnotes can contain full bibliographical information, especially if no proper bibliography appears at the end of the text. Usually, however, footnotes contain information in an abbreviated form which refers the reader to the bibliography at the end.

As you will find these abbreviations very frequently, it is necessary to understand the short forms that are used in footnotes.

REMEMBER: Italic type in printed texts is the same as underlining in typed or handwritten texts.

EXERCISE 7.14

The following words, phrases and abbreviations are frequently used in footnotes in textbooks and journals. Most good dictionaries explain their meaning. So, look up each one in your dictionary, and write down their precise meaning.

anon	ed.	MS., MSS.	tr., trans
ca	et al.	op. cit.	*vide*
cf.	ibid.	*passim*	viz.
ch., chs	l., ll.	*sic.*	vol., vols

EXERCISE 7.15

Read through these footnotes, and then answer the following questions.

1 Shaver, H., 1977, *Malaria and the Political Economy of Public Health*, pp. 557–9.

2 Ibid., p. 623.

3 Ibid.

4 Calder, R., 1964, *Two Way Passage: A Study of the Give and Take of International Aid*, *passim*.

5 Shaver, op. cit., p. 563.

6 Cf. in this connection the work of P. Goubert.

7 Djukanovic, V., et al., 1957, 'Alternative Approaches to Meeting Basic Health Needs in Developing Countries', *WHO Technical Report*, no. 392, p. 6.

8 Jackson, R. (ed.), 1960, *Preventative Medicine in World War II*, vol. I, p. 47.

9 Ibid., vol. II, p. 69.

10 Edmonds, R. T., 1983, 'The Ineffectiveness of DDT Residual Spraying in the Jordan Valley', MS, University of Amman.

(a) What is the title of the work referred to in footnote 3?
(b) Why are these references not in alphabetical order?
(c) Did Djukanovic write all of *WHO Technical Report*, no. 392?
(d) What is the title of the book referred to in footnote 5?
(e) When was the book referred to in footnote 9 published?
(f) Why is the title of the work referred to in footnote 10 not in italics?
(g) Is it likely that the article referred to in footnote 10 will be in your library? Why?
(h) Which of the books by P. Goubert has the writer referred to?
(i) Why is there no reference to a page number in footnote 3?

UNIT 8

Examination Skills

Examination time is the most worrying time in a student's life. It is a time when good planning is perhaps more important than at any other time. Part 1 will give you some hints on **revising**, while Part 2 will tell you about actually **doing the exam**.

PART 1

Revising for Examinations

Here are some Golden Rules for successful revision.

GOLDEN RULE—1

Do not cut classes near exam time so that you can do your own revision.

Are you one of those students who are tempted to skip classes whenever a major assignment is due, because of pressure of work? If you are, you are probably also tempted to give up classes as you come near the end of term, when exams are due, and there seems no time left for revision. You think that you're not being lazy, just giving yourself more time to complete the work.

If you are tempted to do this, **don't!**

The last sessions before any major assignment or any examination are perhaps the most important ones of all. These last lessons will almost certainly be taken up with revision or will contain matters that the tutor considers important enough to mention at the last minute.

Think about it. Which do you think is more likely to be useful for a coming exam: the revision that you think is important, or the revision that the tutor thinks is important?

The answer is obvious, isn't it?

GOLDEN RULE—2

Establish a special revision timetable for yourself, AND STICK TO IT!

Give yourself a certain amount of time for each of the subjects for which you will be sitting, and try to finalize your notes for each one.

209

As you will be under quite a lot stress at this time, it is most important that you allow yourself some time off while you are revising. Plan on having *at least* a half-day off each week. If your institution allows you sufficient time for revision, then plan on *a full day off each week*. This sounds like a lot of time wasted, but the last thing you want to do is to go into the examination room too mentally exhausted to think!

GOLDEN RULE—3

Work through some old examination papers.

Try to find some recent examination papers in the subjects you are to be examined on, and work through them, to see if you can do the answers. There is no need to write out the answers in full, but see if you can answer the questions in note form.

GOLDEN RULE—4

Do not spend the night before the exam trying to cram in more revision!

If you don't know your work by the night before the exam, you never will. A good night's sleep is far more valuable than hours trying to learn what you should have learned weeks ago!

PART 2

Pacing Yourself in the Examination

When anyone sets an examination, he or she is testing whether the students have mastered certain facts or skills that have been taught in the course. **An exam is there to show just how much you have learned**. If you want to score high marks in any exam, you have to **play the numbers game**.

What does this mean? Well, you should always remember that the markers of examinations deal with numbers that eventually must be translated into a **percentage**. Often the writer of the examination will indicate on the examination paper exactly how many marks each question is worth. If you add up these marks, they will always come to either exactly a hundred marks, or a clear fraction of a 100 (10, 20, or 50). If no marks are shown next to each question, then it is safe to assume that each question in the exam is worth the same number of marks.

The value of playing the numbers game is that **you can work out just how much time you should spend on each question,** and, as an extension of this, **just how many items of information you should put in to each of the questions to score the maximum marks.**

Let's look at first of these, as it the more obvious of the two.

Planning the Time Available for Each Question

Look at the mark allocation for the following examinations:

Examination A　　　Time: 3 hours

Question 1	(10 marks)
Question 2	(20 marks)
Question 3	(20 marks)
Question 4	(50 marks)

Examination B　　　Time: 3 hours

Question 1	(5 marks)
Question 2	(10 marks)
Question 3	(10 marks)
Question 4	(25 marks)

Both of these examinations are similar. The only difference is that the *total marks* are 100 for one, and 50 for the other. If you have to spend three hours on each examination, you should spend **the same proportion of your time** on each question of Examination A as you would on Examination B.

You should plan your time in both these exams in the same way:

1 Allow time at the beginning for reading carefully through the paper and, if you are given a choice, deciding which questions to answer. Allow time at the end for tidying up your answers and for checking through for legibility and for the correctness of your English.
2 Divide the remaining time according to the marks available for each question. If there are no marks mentioned on the exam paper, then this is an easy task: simply divide the time available by the number of questions you have to answer. If marks are mentioned, then the situation is a little more complicated.

Look at how this should be done:

For Examination A **and** *Examination B*

Total Time Available: 180 mins

Reading the examination paper:	15 mins
Tidying up at the end:	15 mins
	= 30 mins

Time left for writing the answers: 150 mins

Question 1 (10% of 150)	15 mins
Question 2 (20% of 150)	30 mins
Question 3 (20% of 150)	30 mins
Question 4 (50% of 150)	75 mins

EXERCISE 8.1

How good are you at the numbers game?

Look at the following examinations, and decide how long you should spend on each question.

REMEMBER: Leave time at the beginning and end for reading and checking.

Examination C   Time allowed: 3 hours
Question 1   (15 marks)
Question 2   (15 marks)
Question 3   (20 marks)
Question 4   (25 marks)
Question 5   (25 marks)

Examination D   Time allowed: 3 hours
5 questions   (no marks allowed)

Examination E   Time allowed: 1 hour
Question 1   (20 marks)
Question 2   (20 marks)
Question 3   (30 marks)

Having worked out how you will plan your time throughout the examination, **do not spend more than the allowed time for each question.**

If you haven't finished a question by the time the number of minutes is up, then leave it. Leave a good gap and then go on to the next one. If you spend ten minutes over your allowed time finishing one question, then you have ten minutes less to complete the next question. As we shall see in the next part of this unit, that is a *very* unwise thing for you to do!

If you do not have time to finish a question and you leave a space in the answer booklet, you can always go back and write some more at the end of the exam, when you may well have time left to spare.

PART 3

Where the Marks Come From

Why is one question worth ten marks, while another is worth twenty?

Why has the person who set the exam decided that one question should carry more (or fewer) marks than the next?

The answer to both these questions should be obvious: **it is because the person who set the exam thinks that there is more to say about some questions than others**.

So you, the examination candidate, must write more in the 20-mark questions than in the 10-mark ones. Obvious, isn't it?

What does 'more' mean?

The simplest way of deciding exactly what you should do with, say, a 10-mark question, is to try to decide just how many items of information the examiner might be looking for.

The person marking the exam will be looking for things to tick—and each tick will have to be worth a number of marks. Think how easy it is to divide that ten points into smaller numbers.

1 **Will go into ten ten times—ten items need to be discussed.**

2 **Will go into ten five times—five items needed.**

3 Won't go into ten. (It is unlikely that $3\frac{1}{3}$ items are needed!)

4 Won't go.

5 **Will go into ten twice—two items needed.**

6 Won't go.

7 Won't go.

8 Won't go.

9 Won't go.

10 **Will go only once.** However, it is *most* unlikely that you will be asked to make only one point in a question worth ten per cent of the marks.

If you look at the list, you can see that there are very few possibilities. To score the maximum amount for a question worth ten marks, you are going to have to make either *ten* points, *five* points, or *two* points. Your knowledge of the course and of the tutor concerned are needed here!

> Try the same thing with a question worth *thirty marks*. What are the most likely number of points you are going to have to make to score thirty marks?

This is a very valuable exercise, for it shows you what you have to do to score the maximum number of marks available. If your tutor is looking for ten items and you only write seven, then you can only score seven out of ten for that question! .

How are you going to make these points? Let's look at some sample exam questions and see how you could do it.

REMEMBER: You don't need to know the answers to the questions to do this.

A From a law examination

Identify (but briefly) some significant differences between the English Westminster System and the government established by the Constitution of *one* developing nation.
(5 marks)

How many differences do you think the examiner might be looking for?

B From a psychology examination

Discuss what you have learned about organizational psychology from your field trips to factories. Make specific reference to organizational concepts which relate to the field situation.
(10 marks)

How many organizational concepts might you need to refer to?

C From a geography examination

Discuss how small farming systems in the South Pacific have been influenced by modern technology.
(10 marks)

How many influences should you discuss?

Sometimes questions are split up into even smaller parts.

D From a sociology examination

As a change agent you will be involved with a variety of processes to help bring about change in the situation of the individual, the group or category of individuals and the community.

Discuss how you might work as a case worker, group worker *and* community worker in order to bring about change in the situation of young physically disabled people.
(30 marks)

Here you have *three* tasks: presumably each one is equally important. How many points should you make in your discussion for each of the three roles?

What to Do If You Haven't Time to Finish a Question

By now you should have realized that the purpose of any examination is **to show the examiner what you know about the topics covered in the course**.

If you didn't have time to finish a question in the time allowed by you, there should still have been that fifteen minutes at the end that you left for proofreading.

What if there isn't enough time even then?

REMEMBER TWO IMPORTANT FACTS:

1 The examiner is looking for things to tick.
2 The examiner isn't an ogre who is determined to make you fail! Despite what most students think, teachers at any level do not like failing students. This is worth bearing in mind!

If there really isn't time to write out that essay in full, then **write out everything you still want to say by putting it down in a list, or in note form**.

If you just stop when you run out of time, then there is no possible way for the examiner to give you any more marks than you have earned so far. If you show the examiner what else you would like to say, then at least there is the possibility of getting more marks.

This is the reason why you MUST attempt all the questions that the paper instructs you to answer. If the paper says to answer five questions, and you only answer four, then you can only get four-fifths of the available marks. Even an Albert Einstein will only get a mark of 80 per cent if he only answers four out of five questions in an exam!

EXERCISE 8.2

On the next page is an entire examination paper for a university sociology course. Even though you may know nothing at all about sociology in general, and rural sociology in particular, you can still **plan** how to approach a paper like this, by playing the numbers game.

TRY IT!

Do it like this: decide

(a) how much time you should spend on each question;
(b) how many items you should include for each question.

Note: You don't have to be able to actually answer the questions to do your planning!

FINAL EXAMINATION—SECOND SEMESTER
COURSE—APPLIED RURAL SOCIOLOGY

Time: 3 hours
Instructions to candidates: Answer *all* the questions.

SECTION A

1 Explain briefly what is meant by *five* of the following terms. Give examples to illustrate your definition.
 (a) social articulation
 (b) small-holder production
 (c) settlement patterns
 (d) structural dependency
 (e) subsidy cycles
 (f) class formation
 (g) subsistence surplus
 (h) capitalist mode of production
 (i) non-market sector
 (10 marks)

SECTION B

2 Identify the constraints to development in one of the other fieldwork areas (*not* your own fieldwork area).
 (10 marks)
3 What are the lessons to be learned from the film *My Brother Wartovo*?
 (10 marks)
4 Why is the history of the introduction of agriculture important for rural development in any *one* Pacific country today?
 (10 marks)

SECTION C

5 How does an understanding of changing values, attitudes and family social structures assist in planning for rural programmes? In your discussion refer to *Rural Society* and other readings, and give examples to illustrate your answer.
 (20 marks)
6 Discuss the limitations of 'rapid rural appraisal'. How might some of these limitations be overcome? Refer to your own fieldwork findings, class lectures and readings.
 (20 marks)
7 Outline some of the problems facing women in agriculture today in *one* developing country.
 (20 marks)

PART 4

Deciding What Sort of Answer Is Required

Look at the examination paper again. As shown below, write the words that *indicate* how you must approach each question. The first has been done to show you what is required. Do the same for each question.

    Do you know what each of these words or phrases mean? Below each word or phrase that you have written, write out what you have to do. If you are not sure what the words mean, look back to Part 1 of Unit 6: Writing Skills—you will find them there.

Question 1

Instruction word: 'Explain'.
To answer the question you must: _____

_____

_____

Try to obtain several exam papers from last year. It will help if these papers are from the same courses that you are taking at present.

a Go through the papers, playing the numbers game.

REMEMBER: There are two parts to the game. You should work out:
(a) the amount of time you should allot to each question;
(b) the number of items you should introduce to gain the greatest number of ticks.

    If you find this particularly difficult with any of the papers, then **go to the tutor who teaches you for that particular subject and *ask* for clarification on how to do the paper.**

    It is better to do this now, with last year's paper, than find out there are problems when you are actually sitting in the exam room with this year's paper in front of you!

b Having planned your time allotments and seen how much you need to say for each question, see if you can provide the right amount of information for each question.

Just as with Part A, if you have difficulties doing this with any of the papers, then **go to the tutor who teaches you for that particular subject and *ask* for clarification on how to do the paper.**

Bibliography of Sources

Books

Bright, J. A. & McGregor, G. P., 1970, *Teaching English as a Second Language*, UK, Longman.

Cartwright, Frederick F., 1972, *Disease and History*, UK, Hart-Davis.

Cole, J. P., 1983, *Geography of World Affairs* (6th edition), UK, Butterworth.

Deane, Phyllis, 1967, *The First Industrial Revolution*, UK, Cambridge University Press.

Earle, Peter (ed.), 1974, *Essays in European Economic History 1500–1800*, UK, Clarendon Press.

Eltis, W. A. & P. J. N. Sinclair, 1981, *The Money Supply and the Exchange Rate*, UK, Oxford University Press.

Gill, Colin, 1985, *Work, Unemployment, and the New Technology*, UK, Basil Blackwell.

Gretton, J. & Harrison, A., 1982, *How Much Are Public Servants Worth?*, UK, Basil Blackwell.

Hill, John, 1982, *From Subservience to Strike*, Australia, University of Queensland Press.

King, J. E., 1980, *Readings in Labour Economics*, UK, Oxford University Press.

Milward, Alan S., 1984, *The Economic Effects of the Two World Wars on Britain*, 2nd edition, UK, Macmillan.

Ooi Jin Bee, 1982, *The Petroleum Resources of Indonesia*, Kuala Lumpur, Oxford University Press.

Ramage, Janet, 1983, *Energy: A Guidebook*, UK, Oxford University Press.

McArthur, Tom, 1987, *The Written Word*, Book 2, UK, Oxford University Press.

Smith, Olivia, 1984, *The Politics of Language 1791–1819*, UK, Clarendon Press.

Ward, Ida C., 1962, *The Phonetics of English*, UK, Heffer.

Wilkins, D. A., 1976, *Notional Syllabuses*, UK, Oxford University Press.

Journals

Australian Economic Papers, 24(45), 1985.
Discover, Dec. 1986.

Economist, 28 March, 18 April 1987.

ELT Journal, 39(1), 1985 and 43(3), 1989.

Energy, 11(6), 1986.

Far Eastern Economic Review, 2 August 1984.

Geographical Magazine, July 1986.

Journal of International Studies, 15(1), 1986.

Journal of Modern History, 56(1), 1984.

Journal of the Polynesian Society, 95(4), 1986.

Journal of the Royal Australian Historical Society, 70, part 1, June 1984; 72, part 2, October 1986.

Journal of the Science of Food and Agriculture, 38(3), 1987.

Millenium: Journal of International Studies, 15(1), 1986.

New Internationalist, nos 89, 90, 1980.

New Scientist, 18 July 1985; 22 Jan., 2 April 1987.

Oxford Economic Papers, 37(2), June 1985.

World Health, Aug./Sept. 1986.

Indexes

INDEX 1

Basic Skills Cycles

Some of the more important basic skills in this book are reintroduced several times so that they may be reinforced effectively. The following list indicates how these skills are recycled through the course.

Note: Unit number is given first in **bold**, followed by Part number(s) in *italics*.

INDEX 2

Skills

Note: Unit number is given first in **bold**, followed by page numbers.

INDEX 3

Exercises

Note:
1 Titles in inverted commas (' ') are the titles of journal articles, quoted in their entirety, that are used as part of exercises in the text.
2 Titles in *italic print* are the titles of books, or of journals (whose articles are quoted) that are used as part of exercises in the text.
3 Unit number is given first in **bold**, followed by page number(s).

INDEX 4

Topics in Reading Passages

Note: Unit number is given first in **bold**, followed by page number(s).

Tables 5.1, 5.2 (major food producers)
6, 131, 134, 136

Health care

'African Immunization Year, 1986', *World
Health*, Aug./Sept. 1986, pp. 22–3 **4**, 86

Women

'Women—The Facts', *New Internationalist*, no.
89, 1980, pp. 10–11 **7**, 164, 168–9, 170
'Women Work Twice as Hard as Men', *New
Internationalist*, no. 89, 1980, pp. 20–1
7, 158–60
'Women's Work—The Facts', *New Internationalist*, no. 90, pp. 10–11, 1980 **7**, 170

Youth

'Nailing the Mercury', *Economist*, 18 April
1987, p. 51 **4**, 84